Using Voice and Movement in Therapy

of related interest

Therapeutic Voicework
Principles and Practice for the Use of Singing as a Therapy
Paul Newham
ISBN 1 85302 361 2

Using Voice and Song in Therapy
The Practical Application of Voice Movement Therapy
Paul Newham
ISBN 1 85302 590 9

Foundations of Expressive Arts Therapy
Theoretical and Clinical Perspectives
Edited by Stephen K. Levine and Ellen G. Levine
ISBN 1 85302 463 5

Authentic Movement
Essays by Mary Starks Whitehouse, Janet Adler and Joan Chodorow
Edited by Patrizia Pallaro
ISBN 1 85302 653 0

Discovering the Self through Drama and Movement
The Sesame Approach
Edited by Jenny Pearson
ISBN 1 85302 384 1

Movement and Drama in Therapy, Second Edition
Audrey G. Wethered
ISBN 1 85302 199 7

Poiesis
The Language of Psychology and the Speech of the Soul
Stephen K. Levine
ISBN 1 85302 488 0

Using Voice and Movement in Therapy

The Practical Application
of Voice Movement Therapy

Paul Newham

Jessica Kingsley Publishers
London and Philadelphia

First published in the United Kingdom in 1999 by
Jessica Kingsley Publishers Ltd
116 Pentonville Road
London N1 9JB, England
and
325 Chestnut Street,
Philadelphia, PA 19106, USA.

www.jkp.com

Copyright © 1999 Paul Newham

Library of Congress Cataloging in Publication Data
A CIP catalog record for this book is available from the Library of Congress

British Library Cataloguing in Publication Data
A CIP catalogue record for this book is available from the British Library

ISBN 1 85302 592 5

Printed and Bound in Great Britain by
Athenaeum Press, Gateshead, Tyne and Wear

Contents

Acknowledgements

I would like to acknowledge my appreciation to the following people. Mary Law for bringing to this work such stability and inspired management at the core, enabling me to write this and without whom I would not have been able to. Jessica Kingsley Publishers for their unwavering support and commitment. Jenny Lloyd for providing all illustrations with the exception of Figures 3.3, 3.6, 4.1, 4.2, 4.3, 4.4, 4.5, 4.6, 4.7 and 7.2. Rivcom Publishing Services for producing Figures 3.3, 3.6, 4.1, 4.2, 4.3, 4.4, 4.5, 4.6, 4.7 and 7.2. Nick Hale for taking photograph 7.4. Philip Grey for taking all photographs except 5.1 and 5.2. Alan Robertson for printing all photographs except 5.1, 5.2 and 7.2. Anthony Crickmay for taking and printing Photograph 5.1. Helen Baggett for taking and printing Photographs 5.2 and 7.2. Josephine for keeping Sunday lunch at the Village sacred in the face of pressure.

This book is dedicated to Mary Law, Greg Campbell and Christine Isherwood for support and anchorage in rocky seas.

Voice Movement Therapy – Towards an Integrated Model of Expressive Arts Therapy

Over the past 15 years I have been developing a systematic methodology for using singing and vocalisation as a therapeutic modality. On a personal level, I think the genesis of my work originates in the acoustic cacophony of my childhood, where the angry vocal yells of my father and the sorrowful vocal cries of my mother provided the musical accompaniment to my days. On a professional level, my investigative work began with my search for a way of developing liberated vocal self-expression in people with severe mental and physical handicaps who could not speak but who produced a broad spectrum of non-verbal sounds.

Alone and without a model for what I was attempting to do, I spent many years crawling along the floor, gurgling, screeching, singing and mirroring the many sounds which my clients made in order that I might enter into their language rather than seeking to demand that they speak mine.

I found that with patience and an experimental spirit I could release a certain amount of muscular tension and facilitate a more liberated use of the voice in people whose verbal proficiency was limited or non-existent. With this vocal release my clients seemed also to access a certain positive emotional expression and an attitude of celebration, as though a certain anguish had been assuaged. The question then was what to do with these voices which emerged.

Simultaneously with my investigations into voice with handicapped people, I was working as a composer and vocalist, drawing inspiration and influence from a multi-cultural musical perspective. As my knowledge of the world's music broadened I began to hear parallels between certain vocal qualities in indigenous singing styles, particularly those of the East and

Middle East, and the sounds made by my handicapped clients. Taking short frozen moments from a variety of singing styles and comparing them with short recordings of handicapped voices, I realised that it was often not possible to tell which was which. I then began to produce performances with my clients which choreographed their movements and orchestrated their vocal sounds to create impressionistic theatre pieces.

By combining my artistic research with a study of physiology, I began to evolve a method for using singing as a mode of artistic expression and therapeutic investigation with non-verbal populations. But the key to my work was the use of my own voice as a probe and a mirror. I learned to expand radically the tonal range and timbral malleability of my voice and use this instrument to communicate with my non-speaking clients. Though we could not speak with one another, we could sing – taking singing in its broadest sense. As my work expanded I was increasingly asked to train other professionals to make use of my methods and I gradually began to withdraw from working directly with handicapped people and started to work with professional care assistants, speech therapists, psychologists and a broad range of workers in the field of special education.

Because the exploration of my own voice had been so central to my investigations, my work with these new so-called 'able' clients took a very practical form. I offered one-to-one voice and singing lessons where the objective was not to produce a beautiful voice but to explore the complete vocal range, valuing all sounds as an authentic expression of the person. However, whereas the main obstacles to liberated vocal expression amongst my original handicapped clients had been neuromuscular, it seemed that my new clientele were inhibited and constricted primarily by psychological issues which manifested in various muscular hypertensions that inhibited and impeded liberated use of the voice. In addition, when I was able to facilitate vocal liberation, new-found sounds were often accompanied by intense emotions which in turn produced new sounds as my clients experienced a spectrum of feelings from deep grief to tumultuous joy, expressed through vocal qualities ranging from guttural base to piercing soprano. I therefore realised that to progress with the development of my work, I had to understand thoroughly not only the physiological nature of vocal expression but also the relationship between voice and psyche. Consequently, I combined a theoretical study of physiology and psychotherapy with the undergoing of my own personal psychoanalysis.

In order to understand in more detail the physiological process of vocalisation I needed to observe the internal workings of my larynx whilst vocalising. I was therefore honoured and grateful when David Garfield-Davies, at that time consultant laryngologist at the Middlesex Hospital, London, offered to make a video stroboscopic recording of my working larynx by threading a fibre optic camera through my nasal passages. This confirmed not only that the techniques I was forging enabled the vocal instrument to increase radically tonal range and timbral malleability, but also that they did so in a way entirely synonymous with healthy methods of voice production. Film of this can be seen on the accompanying video to this book *Shouting for Jericho: The Work of Paul Newham on the Human Voice* (Newham 1997a). Meanwhile, I began to realise that many of the tenets of psychotherapy could be transposed from a verbal to a vocal mode of expression. I believed that I was establishing the idea of singing as therapy.

In time my one-to-one practice grew to include many other kinds of clients besides those who wanted to learn the principles of my work in order to apply it professionally. As my private practice of one-to-one voice sessions grew, I had the opportunity to apply my evolving systematic methodology of vocal work to a broad range of clients, some of whom came in the hope of alleviating physical problems such as constriction, asthma, and stammering, whilst others came for psychological reasons such as shyness, debilitating grief or repressed anger. The systematic approach which I had forged from my work with mentally and physically handicapped people was equally effective with this clientele and the added dimension of acknowledging the psychological significance of the process deepened the work with all clients.

Though each client brought with them into my consulting room unique issues which were worked through and explored not through speaking but through singing, I began to recognise certain approaches, exercises, methods and exploratory investigations which seemed to facilitate authentic vocal expression in all clients, regardless of their unique disposition.

Combining the use of my emerging system of vocal release with a unique personal psychotherapeutic relationship with each individual client I realised that I was creating the foundations for a therapeutic modality which compared to the expressive arts therapies – such as drama therapy and dance therapy – except that the channel of expression was voice and movement. I called this modality Voice Movement Therapy.

At the heart of my work was – and is – a systematic methodology for interpreting vocal sound. This system distils the voice into ten acoustic components which emanate from physiological functioning, which provide a language for describing the voice and which relate to psychological, emotional and artistic expression. This system is described in detail in my book *Therapeutic Voicework: Principles and Practice for the Use of Singing as a Therapy* (Newham 1997b) and is outlined briefly in Appendix 1 of this volume. Because of the difficulty inherent in attempting to describe vocal sounds in written words, I have published a set of audio cassette tapes, *The Singing Cure: Liberating Self Expression Through Voice Movement Therapy* (Newham 1998) which explain the Voice Movement Therapy System of Vocal Analysis giving ample vocal examples of the spectrum of vocal sounds in speech and song which arise from different combinations of the ten core ingredients. Details of how to obtain accompanying resources to this book and access other information regarding Voice Movement Therapy is given in Appendix 2 of this volume.

Before long, I had more clients and more work than I could possibly handle. I therefore considered that I could actually reach more clients by training others to impart the work as facilitators, voice coaches, singing teachers, therapists, special education workers and community leaders; so I began running short courses in the techniques and methodologies which I had forged.

In the summer following the first series of short courses, I became unable to work due to exhaustion, and a graduate of one of my training courses, Jenni Roditi, offered to take over my client practice; and in so doing she verified that the techniques were indeed grounded and practicable enough to be passed on and administered by others with equal efficacy as when administered by myself.

On returning to teaching the courses which I was developing and as I observed graduates apply the work in various settings I began to be convinced that there was a need for more trained and qualified practitioners who could use voice to facilitate a therapeutic process which yielded liberated self-expression in others. I therefore developed the short courses which I had been teaching into a full professional training leading to a professional Diploma in Voice Movement Therapy, which is currently accredited by Oxford and Cambridge Universities and the Royal Society of Arts Examinations Board. The major focus of my work is now directing this professional training in Voice Movement Therapy and teaching other short courses in specific areas of the work.

The professional training course in Voice Movement Therapy provides a thorough practical, experiential and technical education in an approach to working therapeutically with the voice which synthesises the physiological, artistic, psychological and educational aspects of vocal work in a single strategy. Because of its broad but integrated nature, it has attracted students from many backgrounds from all over the world. Trainees include musicians and performing artists seeking to develop their vocal and compositional skills; psychotherapists seeking to incorporate vocal work into their approach; speech and language therapists seeking an integrated and experiential model to complement their allopathic training; free-lance peripatetic group leaders who run workshops and offer sessional work for a variety of client groups; and many others whose professional intention is unclear but who seek a personal vocational training which unites exploration of the Self with the acquisition of technical skills. The diverse student fraternity provides a particularly fertile environment and graduates utilise the work in very different ways. Some graduates work with clients or patients in clinical institutions or in one-to-one practice; some devise performances and lead experiential workshops; some offer vocal training in drama schools and in individual client practice; some combine the vocal work with other arts therapies or with physical therapies; and others work in a way that combines a number of different models.

Although the designing and teaching of this course in many ways provided a culmination to my intentions, there was still a missing link. For, on graduating from the training course, practitioners encounter many complex issues relating to the practice of Voice Movement Therapy for which they need further support, supervision, guidance and a sense of being part of a network. I therefore formed the International Association for Voice Movement Therapy which is governed by a code of ethics and a constitution and to which qualified graduate practitioners of Voice Movement Therapy belong. This Association is in its early days but provides an entirely necessary forum for the supervision of practitioners and an investigation of issues relating to the practice of a therapeutic approach to vocal expression.

In seeking to ground Voice Movement Therapy practically and theoretically, I have been driven to research thoroughly the cross-cultural evolution of a therapeutic approach to vocal expression from ancient shamanic practices and spiritual healing to avant garde theatre and present-day psychotherapy; and my research has uncovered a rich history of investigation into the healing use of singing and non-verbal vocal expression in many areas and through many ages. This research has enabled me to develop a consolidated body of vocal work which synthesises the practical application of principles drawn from a range of disciplines including psychotherapy, massage, remedial voice training, stress management, singing, music, ethnomusicology and special needs education. The discovery of other previous approaches enabled me to understand what I was doing as the synthesising of fragments emanating from an existing tradition.

Being sceptical of anything which claims to be new and having a deep respect for tradition, I felt determined to ensure that I brought the long-standing practice of a therapeutic approach to vocal expression to the attention of present-day practitioners and students within the relevant professions. I was therefore honoured when Jessica Kingsley invited me to publish a complete and unabridged history of the use of voice and singing in therapy. In this book, *Therapeutic Voicework: Principles and Practice for the Use of Singing as a Therapy* (Newham 1997b), I have described the theoretical and practical history of the subject. In addition, throughout *Therapeutic Voicework* I have related the various historic and extant approaches to vocal expression to the techniques of Voice Movement Therapy. However, the description of the practical techniques which I have evolved are a marginal part of what is primarily a historical and theoretical overview of the field.

In this book, *Using Voice and Movement in Therapy: The Practical Application of Voice Movement Therapy*, I intend to speak in quite a different voice. This book is the first of a series of three volumes which concern the practical application of Voice Movement Therapy. These books will be a description of Voice Movement Therapy for those interested in the nitty gritty of using voice and movement as a therapeutic tool. For it has come to my attention over the past few years that there is an ever increasing interest in the therapeutic value of singing and non-verbal vocal expression amongst therapists from all orientations. Such professionals and students of the therapies are often eager to have an insight into how a therapeutic modality with singing and voice at its centre actually works in practice. In this book and the two volumes which follow, I shall seek to throw some light on this enquiry and I hope that those seeking to acquaint themselves with an integrated and coherent model of therapeutic vocal work may find inspiration, information and affirmation. Readers interested in the historic and theoretical background are referred to my earlier book *Therapeutic Voicework* (Newham 1997b).

Most therapists, teachers and other practitioners working with the hearts and souls of other people recognise that the human voice is a primary medium of communication in human beings. It is an expression of who we are and how we feel. In the timbre of a person's voice you can hear the subtle music of feeling and thought. The ever shifting collage of emotions which we experience infiltrates the voice with tones of happiness, excitement, depression and grief. The human voice is also one way in which we preserve our identity; and the voice and the psychological state of an individual mutually influence each other. The physical condition of the body is also reflected in the vitality of vocal expression: illness, physical debilitation and habitual muscular patterns all take their toll on the way we sound. The voice is both an expression of psychological state, a physiological operation and the means by which a person asserts his or her rights within the social order. But many people find themselves negatively affected by psychological dynamics such as stress, anxiety and depression, by physical factors resulting from congenital conditions, illness, injury or bodily misuse and by socially enforced inhibitions. If these effects continue unabated, they often begin to reduce the agility and vitality of body and voice and thereby deplete the capacity for unencumbered expression.

Because the voice is composed of such a complex set of dimensions, the condition of vocal inhibition, restraint or depleted function, from which so many people suffer, leads to an expressive impairment on a psychological, physiological and social level. Reversing the process and reviving vocal function therefore necessitates attention to both psychological, physical and social processes. Providing these processes are properly understood, working with the voice can be an enlivening way of helping people overcome difficulties which hinder the acoustic and kinetic expression of the Self. And such work may be called Voicework.

Voicework may perhaps best be described as a generic term which includes any work with or on the voice. Within this definition a singing teacher could be said to practise Voicework in developing the vocal skills of her pupils; a bereavement counsellor could be said to practise Voicework in helping a client feel safe and comfortable in giving voice to grief; a speech and language therapist conducts Voicework in helping a patient be relieved of pathological conditions which threaten the health of the voice; a choir leader may be said to practise Voicework in enabling a mass of disparate voices to synthesise into a harmonious whole; a gestalt psychotherapist may draw upon Voicework in assisting a client to give vent to rage through shouts and yells; a *répétiteur* conducts Voicework when she helps an anxious opera singer with the task of sustaining the demands of the music whilst articulating the poetic text; a music therapist uses Voicework when she helps a young child create a song from a simple rhyme; a priest employs Voicework when using the tonal contours of his voice to communicate to the congregation; a politician uses Voicework when he deliberately employs specific vocal timbres to convince and persuade.

All of these people are using the voice as a channel through which to express or 'push out' something from the inside; and the voice is indeed a major bridge between the inner world of mood, emotion, image, thought and experience and the outer world of relationship, discourse and interaction.

Because the voice is so intimately connected to the expression of feelings and ideas and is a primary channel through which we communicate who we are, Voicework is often innately therapeutic. However, the term 'Voicework' is not synonymous with 'voice therapy'.

The term 'voice therapy' denotes a clinical allopathic field of work conducted by 'voice therapists' who are speech and language therapists with a specialisation in voice disorders. It is also true, however, that a number of medical doctors who have specialised in ear, nose and throat dysfunction and disease (ENT) and who have a special focus on laryngological problems may also call themselves voice therapists. Both ENT doctors and speech therapists alleviate a wide range of disorders and though both kinds of practitioners approach the voice as a somatic phenomenon, increasing numbers of doctors as well as speech and language therapists are beginning to incorporate attendance to the influence of emotional and psychological factors upon the voice.

Although strictly speaking the term 'voice therapy' designates the aforementioned field, in recent years an increasing number of people working in the broad area of 'complementary', 'alternative' or 'holistic' medicine have utilised the term 'voice therapy' to denote the process by which vocalisation through speech, song and non-verbal sound is used as a means through which to express and explore aspects of the psyche. These practitioners utilise the term 'therapy' for its psychic rather than its somatic implication, inviting comparison with the work of psychotherapists rather than speech and language therapists or ENT consultants. However, few of these practitioners are trained in psychotherapy or counselling; which adds further confusion to the vernacular meaning and signification of the term 'voice therapy'. There are also many artistic practitioners, some of long-standing excellence, particularly within the field of the avant garde experimental theatre, who describe their teaching as being, in part, a therapy. This invites the work of theatre practitioners who impart or facilitate vocal work, such as directors, actors and workshop leaders, to be compared to that of a drama therapist. Yet few of these artists are drama therapists. There are also many individuals working in community centres with so-called handicapped children, in mental health wings of hospitals, in special schools and in the voluntary sector who are 'helping' others towards positive change and thus are working therapeutically. Those who utilise vocal expression as part of their approach may understandably be perceived as disseminating 'voice therapy'; yet few of these people have a therapeutic training or qualification.

The widespread use of the term 'therapy' in general and 'voice therapy' specifically is therefore beginning to denote a broad style of work and a particular kind of outcome rather than identifying someone who is trained and qualified in a therapeutic discipline. Furthermore, the word 'therapy', particularly in the current political climate, is subject to so much scrutiny and currently designates such a broad field that it is, for many, time to consider carefully the variety of meanings which the term has.

My assertion is that all approaches to Voicework can most certainly be therapeutic. Moreover, its therapeutic effects can be somatic as well as psychological. This does not, however, necessarily mean that all Voicework practitioners are therapists or that all approaches to Voicework are therapeutic. In fact, many people have suffered the most abominable anti-therapeutic treatment in the hands of voice coaches, singing teachers and voice workshop leaders who, whilst artistically and technically competent in the field of voice, have not the slightest insight into the foundations of compassion and analysis upon which a truly therapeutic contract is built.

Voice Movement Therapy may be described as a particular approach to Voicework and a specifically crafted form of therapeutic Voicework. Voice Movement Therapy can help people whose expressive activity has been detrimentally influenced by emotional problems, trauma and mental illness, those whose lives have been turned around by the effects of severe injury or the development of diseases such as Multiple Sclerosis, those with congenital conditions such as Cerebral Palsy and Down's Syndrome and those who have been discouraged from asserting or expressing themselves by overpowering and infertile environmental influences. In addition, Voice Movement Therapy can respond to the needs of those whose social or professional predicament places exceptional demands upon the voice, who often find themselves ill equipped to preserve the health and longevity of their vocal instrument and therefore require education and rehabilitation. No less important are those who, whilst healthy and not overtly impeded, can nonetheless discover an increased potential for expression and creativity through singing and sound-making.

If not conducted with skill and expertise, however, Voice Movement Therapy can also be threatening to the health of mind and body; and there are some people for whom any kind of therapeutic Voicework, including Voice Movement Therapy, may not be expedient to the maintenance of health no matter how proficient the practitioner. Consequently, someone practising any kind of Voicework needs to be competent in understanding the psychophysical nature of vocal expression, and in addition must learn to recognise those for whom Voicework is an inappropriate medium through which to work for physical or psychological reasons.

In my view, though there are many resourceful, sensitive and proficient voice practitioners administering many diverse approaches to Voicework, some therapeutic and some not, nonetheless any Voicework practitioner, particularly a practitioner working with an overt therapeutic dimension, should be trained to do so.

All students of the professional training in Voice Movement Therapy undergo a thorough physical and psychological journey in order to facilitate the same in others. In addition, all trainees study both creative, allopathic and psychological models of intervention and analysis. They are thereby trained to be practitioners who can deal effectively with the psychological and physical aspects of vocal expression and who, in suspecting serious pathology of mind or body, will refer the client to an appropriate practitioner.

Voice Movement Therapy can be conducted with individuals and with groups. The clients begin by making their most effortless natural sound whilst the acoustic tones of the voice and the muscle tone of the body are heard and observed. In response to an informed analysis of breathing, sound and movement the practitioner massages and manipulates the client's body, gives instruction in ways of moving and suggests moods and images which the client allows to affect and infiltrate the vocal timbre. The voice is thereby sculpted and animated through a graphic and authentic expression of the Self. In order to facilitate this process, the practitioner also offers pedagogic technical training by which the voice develops in range and malleability; this helps the client find access to sounds which give expression to hitherto dormant aspects of the Self. The result of such Voicework is psychologically uplifting, physically invigorating, creatively rejuvenating and serves to release vocal function from constriction.

As the process unfolds, the client is encouraged and enabled to use creative writing from which lyrics for songs are drawn. The practitioner then helps the client create songs which are vocalised using the broadest possible range of the voice, giving artistic expression to personal material. In addition, the spectrum of voices which are elicited during the process are also used as the basis from which to create characters which symbolise and express different aspects of the Self. Voice Movement Therapy thereby draws on dance, music and drama and in many ways, therefore, provides a model for an integrated expressive arts therapy where creative movement, creative writing, music and theatre are synthesised into a coherent strategy within which all strands are linked by the common thread of the voice. However, Voice Movement Therapy differs from other arts therapies in that it necessarily appropriates a physiological dimension, as the voice is so often the locus for somatic and psychosomatic difficulties – and a complete understanding of vocal expression is not possible without an appreciation of the way the voice functions physiologically.

The techniques which constitute Voice Movement Therapy can, therefore, be loosely divided into three areas. The first of these areas is the use of voice with movement, dance and massage and is covered in this first volume: *Using Voice and Movement in Therapy*. The second area is the use of voice with creative writing and singing, which is covered in the second volume: *Using Voice and Song in Therapy*. The third area is the use of voice with drama and performance, which is covered in the final volume: *Using Voice and Theatre in Therapy*.

These books aim to be both theoretically informative and practically inspiring. For, though the use of Voice Movement Therapy as a mode of therapeutic inquiry, like all disciplines, requires training, there are parts of the Voice Movement Therapy methodology which therapists from other orientations can borrow from, adapt and utilise. I hope that the techniques described in this book will inspire practitioners to broaden their field of enquiry to include vocal expression.

Naturally, the untrained, unconsidered use of vocal expression in a therapeutic context is potentially dangerous; and many of the techniques which constitute Voice Movement Therapy require practical training to know how to administer them. This is not a handbook. At the end of the day, each reader must employ a discernment in keeping with the brevity of the subject's treatment here.

Throughout the book I not only give case studies but also reprint clients' own accounts of their experience of the work; and I am grateful to those who have permitted me to tell their story and quote their words. Nonetheless, names and other details have been altered to preserve confidentiality and anonymity.

CHAPTER I

Spherical Space, Spherical Sound
Investigating the Environment
of Inner and Outer Experience

The Influence of Space

The way we move is influenced directly by the space we move through. Environmental landscape affects and impacts physical mobility. An environment which is damp and cold provokes a very different kind of physical expression to an environment which is dry and warm. People move differently in dim light to the way they move through bright light. In crowds of people our gestures and style of mobility speak a different code to the body language which emerges when we are surrounded by empty space. The ground under our feet influences our walking: sand and cement elicit different steps.

This is a simple statement and very obvious. Yet the relationship between environment and motion is deepened and complicated when psychologically contextualised. The present environment through which a person moves is experienced through the idiosyncratic windows of perception which that person has constructed from experience. Therefore, the same physical environment will affect each person in a very different way. Each of us has learned to respond to the space around us; and this learning is primarily influenced by the nature of the environment in which we spent our early years.

The way infants learn to move through physical space is influenced by their sensate, emotional and psychological experience of that space. An infant learning to crawl and walk in an environment of damp and cold has a different journey to a child moving through a dry and warm landscape. The emotional fabric of the environment is influential also. A child surrounded by a cacophony of emotional conflict has his or her movements shaped by fear and anxiety. Meanwhile, a child moving through a landscape of love and tolerance is more likely to develop a physical expression free from the symptoms of hypertension.

The acoustic fabric of the infant's environment also influences physical muscularity. The surrounding sound forms an audio-phonic enclosure. An acoustic envelope which is harsh, discordant and eruptive penetrates the ears and psyche of the infant in a different way to sounds which are consistent, smooth and enfolding. And the neurological response to sound influences muscle use. How we move is influenced by what we hear.

As we grow to adulthood, a vestige of this early environment of infancy is carried with us, surrounding us wherever we go. Although we move through the actual physical space of our environment as it is at any moment, we are also enclosed by the memory of early space. This space is like a little world which surrounds our body 360 degrees; it is a sphere of influence or a kinesphere. As we bend, curl and turn, so the spherical space of our personal envelope bends, curls and turns with us (Figure 1.1).

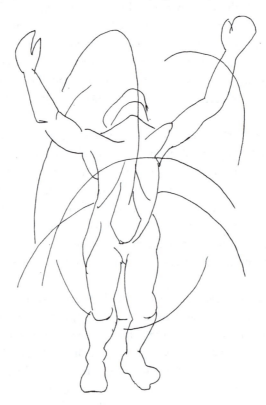

Figure 1.1

The anxieties, fears, worries, insecurities and the sense of safety, security and consistency which constituted the play-room stay with us. Our adult world is, in many respects, still experienced as though we were crawling about in the world of our first home. The first impressions are the hardest to shake off; and the way we move through the world is coloured and impacted by the impressions we formed when we moved through our first environment. The memories of these early experiences are an impressionistic complex of sound, motion and feeling; and the acoustic memories are highly potent, for hearing is the first sense to be stimulated in our development.

Movement in the Womb

The very first space through which we move is, of course, the liquid environment of the womb. A healthy foetus moves inside the womb with a unique choreographic pattern of daily activity which is entirely self-motivated and does not correlate to external environmental circumstances, such as the time of day or to whether the mother is awake or asleep. This movement increases in magnitude and complexity during gestation so that the foetus has already the full repertoire of movements which will be found in the new born baby. This includes the movements which facilitate and accompany breathing and, consequently, vocalisation. The foetus is, therefore, artistically speaking, an improvising solo dancer rehearsing for the impending performance of life.

Visible movement appears at about seven and a half weeks with slow flexing and extension of the vertebral column and passive displacement of arms and legs. Then, at ten weeks, yawns, jaw opening and tongue movements begin to occur regularly as well as sporadic hiccups which reach maximum frequency and magnitude at 13 weeks. Until this point in time during gestation, the tissue cylinder which will become the vocal tract – or voice tube – is passively positioned. With the occurrence of yawning and hiccups, however, the elastic tube which will become the vocal tract is able to lengthen and dilate as well as being able to shorten and constrict.

By 12 weeks, sucking and swallowing are present and are combined with more magnanimous breathing movements which are consistently rehearsed and which reach maximum magnitude at about 30 weeks. Despite this intricate expressive emergence of physiological processes and skeletal muscular movement, the foetus remains mute without any acoustic self-accompaniment; although the foetus is capable of registering and reacting to a range of sounds in the external environment, the voice is released from silence only with the passage from womb to world. Whilst in the womb, where the foetus is completely surrounded by supportive fluid and is enclosed, enveloped and enwrapped in an environment that is dark, wet and sonorous – the ears receive but the voice cannot react.

Viewed from an adult perspective, there is, therefore, a shadow side to this seemingly Utopian container, for it stimulates a foetus who is unable to respond; it reminds us of the dual nature of water which is at once soothing and containing but at the same time drowning and suffocating. Sound too is experienced by the adult as being dual in nature. Sound can bathe us, soothe us and surround us with a calm and undulating ambience; but it can also penetrate, overwhelm and drown us out. This ambivalence is often experienced towards the mother who is perceived as both nurturer and stifler. Despite its shadow, the womb is the safest place the impending infant will ever know; though in later life she will almost certainly attempt to recreate such a safe haven through every means possible.

An astonishing amount of acoustic information passes from the world to the inner terrain of the womb. For example, a newly born infant born in Russia will suckle faster when spoken to in Russian but slower when spoken to in French. A French baby, meanwhile, will suckle faster when spoken to in French. The ears of the gestating foetus are hugely sensitive, not only to the contours of the language spoken on the other side of the abdominal wall, but also to emotional expressions and atmospheres. A mother experiencing depression, anxiety or insecurity influences the growing babe. An environment aloud with sounds of anger and conflict is received by and impressed upon the growing infant. When the baby is born, it already brings with it a certain intrauterine aural history of the world – a world which it sees for the first time but has heard and felt before.

Sound Replaces Water

In the womb, the foetus is surrounded by fluid. But, once the baby is born, she loses the sense of this liquid which surrounds her 360 degrees; from now on the only aspect of the environment which seems to enclose her so completely is sound.

Sound and water behave in similar ways, they travel multi-directionally filling every crevice and passing through every chink. Unlike the optical field of the infant's vision, which is limited by the angle of the eyes' receptivity to light, the aural field is 360 degrees and sound stimuli can be heard from all directions. For the infant, the sonorous envelope of sound created by both her own crying and the responsive voice of the mother is potentially a perfect replacement for the watery container of the womb, which supported the semi-spherical convex and concave surfaces of the gestating body. One of the reasons babies cry is to recreate this sense of an enclosure which holds and supports. The baby produces a blanket of sound, an acoustic enclosure which enwraps and envelops her as completely as did the amniotic fluid.

The maternal voice also plays an important role in providing a container, an acoustically delineated and boundaried spatial area in which the baby can experiment with the actions that facilitate growth. In addition, the maternal voice provides an acoustic mirror in which the child first hears itself reflected.

Thus, the vocal and physical relationship between mother and child reflects and moulds the child's developing identity. A sense of insecurity experienced by the mother can be communicated to the baby through specific vocal timbres, which may give the baby the impression of a container which is unstable, undefined and frail, impeding the baby's own sense of security. A mother's voice which is too penetrative and abrasive may cause the baby to feel intimidated and overwhelmed. A mother's voice which is too timid may leave the baby without a sense of support. Sound makes space; and the quality of sound in a baby's environment, particularly the orchestration of the mother's voice, colours her experience of that space.

Spherical Space

The degree to which we feel safe, held and supported and the degree to which we feel negatively impeded, threatened and insecure in the womb and afterwards, in the spherical space of the sonorous envelope created between mother and infant, influences the way we will experience every environment through which we move thereafter. As adults, we still, to a certain extent, experience the environment around us as being coloured by the same factors which constituted our early spaces. Consequently, we move as though through our own spherical space which influences our physical and emotional expressions (Figure 1.2).

We can experience the spherical space of another person when we approach them and begin to sense the quality of presence which they radiate. Each person emits a certain atmosphere, a quintessential selfness which is emotionally charged and which influences our perception of their personality. And we can detect this Self before the person has said a word or moved a muscle. Of course, part of the impression we form of someone is influenced by how they look; but blind people who are denied visual

Figure 1.2

appreciation also sense the spherical space around a person and are able to perceive the qualities with which the space is filled. Deaf people, too, sense the spherical atmosphere around someone without needing to hear them. The psychological atmosphere which weaves the fabric of our surrounding spherical space is therefore also 'trans-sensate' – it is beyond the senses. Without this, the kind of projective communication upon which psychotherapy is built would be impossible. For, in psychotherapy, the client and therapist literally 'transfer' psychological material through space and into one another's spherical space and psychological environment. This is called 'transference'.

When we observe people move, then, we are not so much noticing the way the present environment influences their mobility, for the main aspects

Figure 1.3

of people's movement patterns remain consistent through changes of environment. Rather, we are watching the way their invisible spherical space influences their pattern of physical expression. We have to imagine that the person carries with them a sphere which surrounds them 360 degrees and which is populated by fears, anxieties, constrictions and inhibitions, threats and obstacles. For, on the whole, we all experience the most virulent of our psychological troubles as external influences. We feel our problems bearing down on us (Figure 1.3).

Very often, when we observe a person's movement patterns, we see their own psychological difficulties translated into physical environmental factors which then seem to be influencing the body from without. For example, someone driven towards unrelenting achievement by an obsessional and anxious industriousness may translate this into feeling that there is a force in the environment driving them forward. Consequently, they may seem as though they are always situated at the front of their spherical space, for ever driven forward by a persecuting power (Figures 1.4). Another person who may experience themselves as stifled and restricted may seem to move as though in a very tiny spherical space, hunched over from the shoulders and somewhat awkward in their mobility, as though the space around them is too confined. Another person may move tentatively and timidly, side-stepping as they go, as though always on the edge of their spherical space, about to fall over or fall out of themselves (Figure 1.5). Another person may seem to be surrounded by a large spherical space in which they stand at the centre, radiating a confidence but revealing little vulnerability.

Figure 1.4

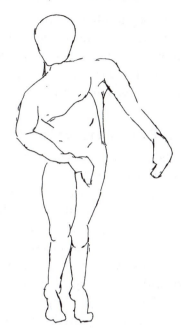

Figure 1.5

Figure 1.6

Voice Movement Therapy involves a series of exercises and explorations which offer clients an opportunity to experience this personal spherical space and to make changes to their psychological environment and the way they express themselves in the space created by their own psychological experience. The first of these processes is called Establishing the Sphere.

Practical Method: Establishing the Sphere

Establishing the Sphere seeks to facilitate in the client the sensation that the space which surrounds the body itself is wombful, fluid, sonorous, all-encompassing and, above all, spherical in shape.

Clients are asked to go to a part of the studio where they feel comfortable. Standing still with arms hanging loosely by their sides they are then asked to imagine themselves to be in the centre of a sphere. Clients are then asked to venture forwards and backwards, side to side, and up and down, making hands-on contact with the imagined internal curved surfaces of the surrounding Spherical Space (Figure 1.6).

Having done this, the client repeats the exercise, focusing particularly on the sensation of standing in the centre of the floor of a sphere. Clients then walk forward, experiencing the fact that with each step forward they also ascend, for the concave nature of the floor rises up before them. As they move back towards the centre they feel a converse descending as the concave floor of the sphere descends behind them. Then, as they move backwards away from the centre they feel an ascending as they imagine walking up the concave floor. They also experience this ascending and descending as they move from side to side.

Throughout the exploration of Spherical Space, clients are asked to imagine that their torso is itself a sphere. Clients are encouraged to breathe in and out through their mouth and are asked to imagine that their mouth is an opening to a tube which passes down into their torso which is filled with air during inspiration and emptied during expiration.

The first aspect which is immediately highlighted in this exercise is the diversity of magnitude between the spheres of different clients. Whilst some create for themselves a sphere which occupies half the studio, others create one so small they barely need to leave the centre to make contact with the extremities. Moreover, the size of the sphere created by clients in ongoing work changes each time the exercise is pursued. It is as though we live in a transient process where the amount of space which is truly ours and in which we can move alters in connection with the transitional flux of our thoughts and emotions. There are times when we are hemmed in, compressed, stifled, and other times when we experience the spaciousness of our personality and Self. There are also times when we seem to limit deliberately the size of our sphere, as though pulling in the boundaries and the limits of our Self for protection and control. This is allegorised in the experience of having more or less room to be heard and in sensations of needing room to breathe. As each client creates for themselves a sphere, the practitioner observes its magnitude which often reflects how much space the client feels there is in which to express herself.

It is useful for clients to imagine that the sphere contains their moods, preoccupations, desires, fears and sensations and that their selfhood does not end at the skin, but also surrounds them. By offering clients this opportunity, the area of psychological reality which is experienced as being around rather than within the somatic container is made palpable.

As clients move through their sphere, it is usual for specific places within it to arouse particular affects, even though the relationship between identifiable geometric points within the sphere and the feelings, moods and sensations aroused by them is different for each person. For example, most clients experience a radical difference in mood when they are close to the back of the sphere compared to that which is provoked by being up against the front surface. For many, the back of the sphere instigates sensations of withdrawal, depression, introversion and fear; whilst for others, meanwhile, it offers security, protection and a sense of confident stability. The front of the sphere for some is unnerving, exposing and feels dangerously unprotected; whilst for others it is experienced as liberating and a place from which they can be seen and heard.

Establishing the Sphere physicalises the sense of Self. This is not surprising given that so much of our self-language is geometrical. We speak of a damaged Self as being 'spaced out' and 'in orbit'; mental anxiety creates a feeling of being 'on the edge'; in depression we feel 'down' and in elation we feel 'up'; our minds go round in circles, we misplace our memories, shelve ideas and bury our desires; we conceive of the unconscious as being located in space beneath consciousness and the spiritual aspirations of the higher self as being vertically above the conscious psyche. In fact, the concept of Self remains verbally inarticulate without recourse to a spatial metaphor. Providing clients with an opportunity to establish and explore Spherical Space gives them a spatial language with which to articulate their own inner process without needing to employ the language of psychological diagnoses.

Case Study: Mary

Big Sphere, Tiny Body

Mary was 52 years old and came into therapy because she had reached a point of extreme frustration at feeling 'worthless', 'unmotivated' and 'unacknowledged'. She also complained of feeling very 'down' most of the time and 'all used up', as though she had no energy left.

When Mary was introduced to Spherical Space, she entered into the process of Establishing the Sphere with enthusiasm and concentration. As I observed her plot out the boundaries of her sphere I was struck by its enormity. She took about five full steps from the centre to draw the surrounding concave walls and when she came to mark out the ceiling she reached as high as she could and seemed still not to have got as high up as she wanted.

Having established the sphere, Mary began to wander aimlessly around. The enthusiasm with which she had established the sphere seemed to have vanished and her body seemed collapsed and hunched over, with her eyes focused towards the floor. Eventually, Mary sat at the back and to the right side of her sphere with her knees up, her chin resting on them, and her eyes focused across diagonally to the left front side of the sphere. Every now and again she would get up, stretch and walk about, but always return to the same position.

After some time, Mary began to tip-toe around the sphere, going up to its extreme edges and peering out as though through a peephole. It looked as if she was hoping to attract someone's attention. Then she would turn around with a look of disappointment on her face and return to her hunched position with her chin on her knees.

Eventually, after repeating this choreography a number of times, Mary rolled over onto her hands and knees and began crawling, looking from side to side. Occasionally she would try to crawl up the walls of the sphere and rub her head against the extremity as though trying to squeeze out.

As with watching all Spherical Space investigations, I noticed myself conceive of various scenarios which helped me imagine a context for Mary's movements. Yet, I also realised that my story and her story would probably be very different.

This is her account of the experience.

Client's Account: Mary

Feeling Small, Feeling Invisible

I enjoyed Establishing the Sphere. I felt as though I was drawing a protective shield around myself that no one could enter and where I could have some peace and quiet. But then, when I had built the sphere, it felt so enormous that I felt like a tiny insect crawling around inside unable to get out. But more frightening was the feeling that if I screamed no one would hear me. I found these feelings quite paralysing so I got myself into a familiar position for me: sitting with my legs up and my chin on my knees.

Then I began to stare into space and realised that this is how I have spent much of my life. My life has been a long series of nursing sick people; I seem to have been cursed with having to look after those around me who have been ill. I have spent hours on a chair next to a bed with my chin on my knees.

No wonder I built such a big sphere, I was trying to create room for 'me'. But, I don't feel that anyone sees me, or even gets a chance to see me, because I am always nursing someone who needs just a part of me. I have felt for many years like I wanted to 'get out' and that I have been screaming inside, but no one has heard. Being in the sphere made me want to scream out loud.

There was also a strange humming and buzzing in my ears as I moved through my sphere. I felt like there was lots of whispering and chattering but that I could not hear what was being said. I felt that I was in the dark and being kept from knowing what was going on. I think I have always felt that the action was somewhere else, that I was missing the party.

One Sphere Many Worlds

The experience which Mary had of Establishing the Sphere was unique to her own disposition, to where she was in her journey at that time; and we will follow Mary's development in response to different therapeutic explorations throughout this book. One of the remarkable things about working with Spherical Space is that it is such a universal and fundamental spatial idea which anyone can grasp and enter into; yet it affords a great deal of room for personal variation, resonance and meaning.

First, everybody has an ongoing relationship with 'their space'. Everyone is aware of having more or less room for the expression of their own personality. The subject of personal space is so integral to the way we think about ourselves. Consequently, working with the idea of a personal psychological space through physical personification gives everybody an opportunity to turn a psychological reality into a sensate experience. Establishing the Sphere and exploring Spherical Space clarifies and brings into sharp relief something which is always subtly present.

Second, everybody has an ongoing relationship with the subject of personal boundaries. The boundaries between our Self and others is primary in shaping the expression of our personality. Some people feel so permeable that their sensitivity can be excruciatingly painful; as though they have no skin. Others feel so 'thick-skinned' that they find it difficult to sense the emotional qualities of others, or indeed of themselves. Many people have had their original boundaries disrespected and invaded through abuse. Others have never really been offered the sacred right to experience a personal sphere of dignity around their Self in the first place.

Establishing the Sphere and exploring Spherical Space provides an opportunity to explore the boundaries between Self and world. As the client plots out the boundaries of their sphere, it is as though they are touring the contours and biology of their psychic skin. Many clients imagine the skin of their sphere to be made of a particular material and to be specifically coloured. From rock to paper, from black to red, every client imagines an idiosyncratic spherical skin which often metaphorises the nature of their own psychic sensitivity, its permeability, its strength and fragility, its colourful vitality and its faded hue.

Here is another example of a personalised experience emanating from Establishing the Sphere.

Case Study: Martin

Trapped and Unbalanced

Martin was 36, was married with two children and worked as a taxi driver. He had come into therapy in the hope of alleviating what he described as his 'stutter' which he had been 'afflicted with on and off' since he was about eight years old. He also wanted to alleviate his recurrent headaches which he was beginning to feel had a psychological significance and cause.

Unlike Mary, when Martin came to work with Establishing the Sphere, he marked out the boundaries of one so small it barely contained him; in fact he only took a step from the centre with one foot at a time to draw out the surrounding concave walls. As he explored a Spherical Space, he seemed almost afraid to wander away from the centre, keeping one leg rooted there all the time.

Having established the sphere he seemed to be quite confident. Then he walked very slowly and very carefully to the front, the back and the two sides. But he seemed to experience the ascending and descending the concave floor so intensely that he kept having to swing his arms to prevent himself from falling over. As he swung his arms, his face took on a horrified expression and his eyes flickered.

As with Mary, I was intrigued at the kind of story I was weaving to explain Martin's movements. In Voice Movement Therapy, the counter-transference – that is the feelings, sensations and images which the practitioner has whilst witnessing a client – is extremely strong. Sound and movement create such resonant images and provoke intense emotional responses. Often, at the core of the counter-transference is an astute intuition which represents an integral part of the client's experience, even though they may have not yet realised it. At other times, the practitioner realises that his counter-transference was miles off the mark and that the client was dealing with something quite other than that which the practitioner had imagined. Because of the spectrum of discrepancy from inspired accuracy to faulty interpretation, I believe it is important to have a sceptical and modest attitude towards one's own counter-transference whilst simultaneously acknowledging what it tells you.

As I watched Martin – again allowing myself to weave my own scenario based on my counter-transference – I had the idea that he was building a booby-trap. He seemed like an inventive professor being consumed and ravaged by his own invention.

This is his account of the experience.

Client's Account: Martin

Falling Upwards

Looking back I did what was typical of me. I don't give myself enough time or enough space. Someone says 'hey man, make a sphere, the world is your oyster'; and I make a tiny eggcup. I feel mad at myself for a missed opportunity.

When I had made my mini sphere, I felt fine standing in the centre, but when I came to move away to the edges, I felt nervous and edgy, as though, like a kid, I wanted to get back home.

I experienced the idea of the curved floor easily. In fact I felt it so much I thought I was going to fall over. But most important to me was what I discovered about my breath. When I was standing in the centre, my breath felt easy and smooth and in fact I wanted to sing or talk or make sound. But when I was away from the centre my breathing felt trapped and I knew that if I was to talk then, I would definitely stutter.

I kept going back and forth between the centre of my sphere and the extremities. As the sphere was so small, this only really took one step. But this was enough to turn my breathing from being easy and fluid to being caught-up and tight. It made me think of how little it takes to get me worked up and anxious, as though something that might seem insignificant to someone else can be a big thing for me.

Because of the effect of the sphere work on my breathing, I had a desire to speak or make talking sounds so I could see how different places in the sphere changed my voice.

Practical Method: Sounding Spherical Space

Martin's desire to make speech sounds and Mary's desire to scream typifies the sensation of wanting to vocalise which many people feel when they begin to work with Spherical Space; and as with Mary we will return to Martin's development in response to different therapeutic explorations throughout this book.

Having established the sphere there is an intense silence which seems to surround the client and the natural tendency is to break this silence with the sounds of the voice. Sound is also experienced within the metaphor of physical space, on a spectrum from high to low. Furthermore, sound is experienced as surrounding the listener 360 degrees, that is, spherically. In the next exploration, called Sounding Spherical Space, clients re-explore the components of Spherical Space which they have, hitherto, experienced mute, accompanied this time by their own vocal utterances. Now, as they move forward and back and side to side, they gently vocalise and are encouraged to begin allowing the lips and the tongue to stop the air flow momentarily, creating consonants and weaving a compositional babble which accompanies the choreographic movement of their body.

Firstly, clients are asked to Establish the Sphere in the same way as before, but making changes to the size and fabric of the sphere in response to the psychological discoveries which they made during the first exploration of Spherical Space. As they move, they are encouraged to breathe evenly and then to vocalise on one note for a few minutes. Then, they are asked to open and close the lips, making sounds such as 'mama' and 'papa'. They are then encouraged to diversify these sounds, composing with vowels and consonants – 'la te boo da go le ma pa'. The resulting acoustic canvas is, musically speaking, like a jazz scats improvisation. Psychologically speaking, it compares to the preverbal babbling stage of infant development.

The atmosphere provoked by this work is usually one of exquisite tenderness and introverted awareness of very primary emotions. It is not uncommon for clients to weep as they work whilst others in the group may be smiling, or laughing. It is important that all concerned are permitted the space to continue working physically and vocally as they experience and express such emotions. This prepares the ground for later vocal work where, like the greatest singers, clients will continue vocalising at their moments of most intense affect.

This is how I observed Martin as he explored Sounding Spherical Space.

Case Study: Martin

Clear Notes and Obstacles

When Martin was standing in the centre of his sphere, he made very quiet, timid sounds with lots of free air. They were long, continuous notes, quite high in pitch.

Then he began combining his cautious trips to the extremities of the sphere and the unbalanced movements which made him look as though he was going to fall over with his gentle vocal sounds to produce a kind of scenario.

He would begin standing confidently in the centre of his sphere making long continuous sounds, without stammering. Then he would begin to walk away from the centre, ascending and descending the imaginal curved floor of the sphere. This would then cause him to swing his arms in order to prevent him from falling and as he did this his sounds would become more rhythmic and intermittent as though he was stammering.

As I watched Martin, I could not help but notice how I experienced a radical change in his demeanour as he passed from uninterrupted clear sounds to rhythmic interrupted sounds. As he moved into his disturbed vocalisation, he seemed to become like a child. The expression on his face was so vulnerable and the feeling I had was of wanting to rescue him. Yet, when he was centred he seemed so mature, so fatherly that I felt almost that he could rescue me. It was as though my counter-transference with him went back and forth from me being his father to me being his son. I thus begun to wonder about his childhood and whether there was a story about to unfold that would give a psychological context for both his headaches and his vocal constrictions.

This is Martin's own account of his experience of Sounding Spherical Space.

Client's Account: Martin

Losing Ground, Losing Voice

I realised that when I was standing in the centre of my sphere I could vocalise with ease and enjoyed the sound I was making. It reminded me of how I feel when I am driving my taxi with no customers in it. I feel centred and in control.

Then, when I began to move out away from the centre, I felt the ground under my feet moving and I did not enjoy the sensation of moving up and down combined with moving forward and back. Being away from the centre made me feel nervous and I felt I was losing my balance. This made my voice wobbly and I began to make sounds which were more like my stuttering voice that I am used to. Then my voice seemed to get stuck and just came out in a series of croaks which didn't sound like me at all.

I also noticed, as I was working, that other people in the group had much bigger spheres than I did. I was struck by this and realised how hemmed in I feel, almost squashed. In fact, one of my nightmares is of having a road accident in my taxi and of being unable to get out of the seat, with metal imploded all around me.

By the end of the exercise I had a headache and my brain inside my head felt the same as I felt inside my sphere: squashed and dizzy.

The Inner Space Without

Martin's experience of feeling hemmed into a Spherical Space which made him feel dizzy was analogous to the way he felt his inner psyche was hemmed into his head. Indeed, many clients find that exploring Spherical Space is a way of exploring how the inner terrain of their body makes itself known. It as though the imaginal skin of the sphere metaphorises their actual epidermal skin; and it is as though their body inside the sphere metaphorises the inner organs of their soma.

Exploring Spherical Space brings to the surface the complex psychological subject of the boundaries between what is inside and what is

Figure 1.7

outside. It also brings home the paradoxical relationship between inner and outer experience which is often not as clear-cut as it seems.

For example, when we dream, we experience ourselves as being inside our dreams, moving through the landscape, interacting and observing. Yet, whilst we are in our dreams, at the same time, our dreams are in us. Dreaming turns space into a paradoxical paradigm where inside and outside are one.

The spatial nature of dreams symbolises our psychic experience. The way we experience the space of our private feelings and thoughts is such that we feel them to be inside of us. Yet, at the same time, we feel that we are in our feelings, often submerged by them as they fall upon us from the outside.

Because the feelings and images which adorn our inner space are so non-palpable, we tend to physicalise them and experience them metaphorised in the environment of outer space. At the same time, because the qualities of the outer environment affect us so deeply, we tend to psychologise them and experience them as being part of our inner world. As we move through the physical world, we therefore carry around us a Spherical Space populated by the kaleidoscopic fragments of past, present and future psychological experience (Figure 1.7).

By understanding the relationship between how we psychologise outer space and how we physicalise our inner space we can, by changing one, change the other.

This is how Martin used Spherical Space to deepen his psychological and physical investigation and make changes to his psychophysical environment.

Client's Account: Martin

Making Room

The next time I worked with Spherical Space I created a much larger one and I moved through it evenly and slowly, breathing deeply. Having built it, I moved away from the centre and walked around, every now and then looking back to the centre. I felt like the big sphere was full of air and I had the sensation of walking along a beach on a windy day. As I began to vocalise, I could feel an easy flow of sound and I managed to vocalise for some time without feeling stuck or stuttered. Then I started thinking about my head and I imagined that inside my skull was a lot of space – the opposite sensation to the one I get when I have headaches. My head felt clear and I realised a simple, obvious yet significant fact: I need space and I don't like pressure.

I then retraced the edges of my sphere, drawing one as small as in my first exploration. I stood at the centre breathing more shallowly and making departures up and down the curved floor. I could feel my breath getting caught and my head getting pressured as I started to wobble and get dizzy. The whole of my body inside the sphere felt like my brain inside my head: crushed and stifled.

To escape this horrible sensation, I gently pushed forward the walls of my sphere, returning it to the more generous size. I began to breathe deeply and move through Spherical Space with the sensation that my brain now had room to expand, room to think. I also felt like my chest had room to expand as I breathed and I felt spacious once again.

I felt amazed that my head, my breath and my whole body as well as my feelings were so different in the small sphere when compared to how I felt in the large sphere. More amazing to me was that I could make such major changes to my breath, my voice, the sensations in my head and my whole body just by altering the dimensions of my sphere. I now felt certain that my headaches and my stutter were related to the way I go through life in a sphere which is not big enough for me. Maybe this is connected to feeling small when I was a kid and of not feeling that I was clever enough to take up space and stick my neck out.

So I now repeated the same journey of making first a large sphere, then a smaller one and then returning to a larger one combined with vocal sounds. And, sure enough, the difference in my voice depending upon the size of my sphere was remarkable.

As I explored, my whole body inside the sphere this time felt like my voice box. It was as though the first time I was my brain in my head and this time I was my voice box in my neck. When the sphere was small, my throat felt caught, tight and constricted and the sounds I made were very interrupted and tense. But when I had a large sphere, my throat felt free and sounds rolled out of my mouth very smoothly. I felt sure that my headaches and my stutter were related but I was not quite sure how.

Space to Voice In

Our sense of space also influences our voice; for giving voice is our way of making the space to be heard. For many people, they feel simply that this space does not exist. For some, their Spherical Space is too small to create any echo or reverberation and their voice seems to be pushed inside of them and corked. For others, their Spherical Space is too big and they feel that their voice is lost in the abyss, like singing into a desert.

The way people experience their voice is also coloured by spatial sensations and a familiar one is of a space that is blocked by an obstacle. Often, people talk about their voice being trapped behind a door, behind a wall or of it being locked inside a chest.

The exploration of Spherical Space magnifies and amplifies these psychophysical sensations. The sphere becomes an imaginal metaphor for the body's boundaries and the client inside the sphere personifies body parts. One of the most frequently personified parts is the larynx and the sensations which the client has inside the sphere are often analogous to the sensations localised in the throat which the client has during vocalisation. This is made particularly intense by the fact that the voice is experienced as a material which passes from the inside of the body to the outside. Voice is something which connects inner and outer environments. The voice also penetrates to the inside of a listener's body and is a means by which we enter one another.

By making changes to the Spherical Space through which they move and to the way that the body feels inside the sphere, clients can consequently transform the way that the voice feels as it passes from the inside to the outside of the body.

This is Mary's experience of Sounding Spherical Space.

Client's Account: Mary

The Silent Scream and the Pathetic Whimper

When I returned to my sphere to explore making sound I was excited at my realisation that I was going to have an opportunity to scream.

I began by tracing out the boundaries of my sphere, only this time I made my sphere a little smaller in the hope that I would not feel so swamped. I then began crawling around like an insect again, as this seemed to sum up how I felt. I began nudging the extremities of my sphere and opening my mouth, making a single tone, gradually increasing loudness.

However, at a certain point, which seemed a lot quieter than I imagined I would be able to go, I seemed to hit a ceiling or an iron door and my voice would neither go higher in pitch nor increase in volume any more.

I felt pathetic, for I was barely making a whimper.

When I listened to this sound I realised that it sounded just like the 'me' I am tired of: pathetic, weary, subservient, gentle and weak. I could do nothing but crawl back into my familiar corner with my chin on my knees and cry. However, as I pondered, I realised that I had not explored any of the space above me. It was as though I was keeping myself down. So, inspired by this realisation, I began making swooping movements with my arms and soon I was jumping up off the floor and spinning around.

I started to turn my focus upwards and as I did, my neck seemed to lengthen and my voice jumped up what felt like at least an octave.

The plate or ceiling which felt as though it had kept me from screaming seemed to slide away and out came this long piercing tone. However, I then got terribly embarrassed and ashamed and immediately returned to my spot on the floor with my chin on my knees.

Repeating the Sphere

Working with Spherical Space is most effective when it is repeated regularly, either in a group or in one-to-one sessions. The verbal discussing and analysing of the experience with the practitioner provides an opportunity for the client to make connections between the physical and acoustic exploration and the potential psychological issues which the exploration reflects.

This means that each time the client returns to work with Spherical Space they take with them more insight and knowledge and are empowered to make different choices which in turn provoke different sensations. This then enables the client to see how alternative choices can be made in the everyday world of interaction and communication. In other words, changing the architecture and acoustics of Spherical Space in the therapy studio provides a template for changes which can be made to the way the client moves and vocalises in their own personal sphere and within the grand sphere of the world at large.

For example, Mary began to realise that she had for so long said yes to so many people's needs that she had to create an enormous sphere to contain everybody and it left her feeling belittled and overcrowded. So, in therapy, she began to establish smaller spheres in which she felt sensations of being tall and contained. In her life, she simultaneously found that she began to make less room for other people and she began to 'close her doors a little bit'. In addition, in therapy Mary began to feel that her sphere was made of sponge, which meant she absorbed every stimulus, particularly the emotions of those in need. As she worked with Spherical Space, she began to explore the notion of Establishing a Sphere made from other, less permeable substances. In her life, meanwhile, this was paralleled by a process of learning to filter the demands made of her by others, in order that she could keep a little of her Self for herself.

In Martin's case, the opposite was true. He had to work to create a larger sphere which gave him room to breathe and vocalise. In his life, this meant taking the courage to widen his circles of interaction beyond the doors of his taxi and the walls of his intimate family life. Mary had too many people in her life. Martin kept himself to himself. In addition, Martin discovered that by imagining that he occupied a larger Spherical Space combined with focusing on breathing into the expansiveness of the inner sphere of his torso, he could decrease the frequency and violence of both his headaches and what he described as his 'stutter'.

Of course, this was by no means the end of the troubles; for Mary or for Martin. In fact, their journeys had only just begun.

CHAPTER 2

Convex and Concave
The Architecture and Acoustics
of Motion and Emotion

The Body's Curves

On the outside, the human body is composed of spherical and semi-spherical surfaces which at points of protrusion are convex and at points of indentation are concave. The eye sockets, the navel and the mouth, the arch of the foot, the crest of the neck beneath the chin, the palms of the hands, the pits of the arms, the backs of the knees and the small of the back – all these are concave. And, their nature is mirrored by the protruding ankles, the balls of the feet, the shins, thighs and buttocks, the belly, breasts and brows, all of which are convex. The human body is a terrain of convex and concave surfaces which glide into one another, curving and turning to produce a semi-spherical architecture. The convex crown of the head glides into the concave indentation in the small of the neck which spreads out to become the convex shoulders. The convex shoulders curve downwards to create the concave indention beneath the arms and this surface curves around to become the convex breasts. The human body is a terrain of curvilinear surfaces which pass eternally through the archetypal graphics of convex and concave (Figures 2.1). This concave and convex nature of the body is choreographically scored deep into the structure of the tissue during the gestating period when the foetus is curled in a position which, at the front of the body, is concave with an indentation at the bottom of the sternum and where the back of the body mirrors this with a convex arch of the spinal column.

The inner environment of the body is also modelled on the sphere where a vital network of spherically walled cylinders transports the elemental liquids and gases to and from the curvilinear organs in order to maintain the life force. Air passes through the cylindrical trachea and bronchi into the semi-spherical lungs; blood flows through the cylindrical veins and arteries,

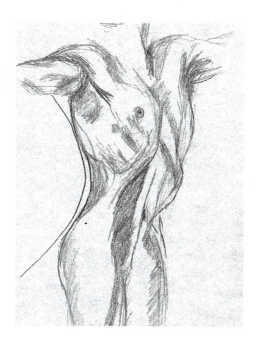

Figure 2.1

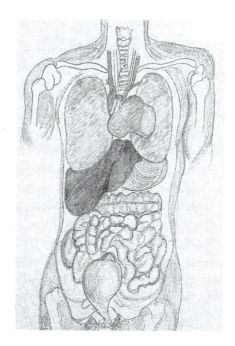

Figure 2.2

Figure 2.3

pumped through the semi-spherical heart; whilst semi-digested food passes from the semi-spherical stomach and through the tubular intestines. The body contains no cubes and no planes; only curves and cylinders (Figure 2.2).

The Convex and Concave Nature of Emotion

Human movement causes a perfect proportional exchange between convex and concave. As one surface of the body becomes convex, so its opposite surface becomes concave to the same degree. As one surface of the body becomes concave, so its opposite surface becomes convex to the same degree. As the back of the hand curves around to grasp a glass, becoming more convex, so the palm of the hand must, by the laws of architectural design, become more concave by the same degree (Figure 2.3). As we move from standing to crouching, the front and rear planes of the torso mirror each other in a convex and concave relationship. As the front becomes more concave so the back becomes more convex to the same degree. No part of the body can move in one direction without its opposite surface moving in mirrored sympathy.

Our emotions also follow this symbiotic ebb and flow between convex and concave. As one part of the psyche becomes filled with joy, so its counterpart on the dark side of the moon moves closer to sorrow. As one surface of the psyche becomes depressed, so its other side moves closer to anxiety.

Jung claimed that as far as the unconscious is concerned, emotions are paradoxical sources of passion; they are not divided into polar opposites. It is the conscious mind that needs to split happiness from sadness, fear from rage. To the unconscious, happiness and sadness are part of the same essence; fear and rage emanate from a single place (Jung 1953).

Many clients come into therapy in order to access, transform or understand particular emotions. For there are many people whose lives are governed by particularly intense emotional experiences. Some feel consumed with depression, some with sorrow; others seem to host inordinate amounts of grief whilst others feel permanently on the edge of rage. Because all emotions are fundamentally connected to their apparent opposite, and because motion influences emotion, working with convex and concave movement patterns can help people reconnect with the mirror image of their familiar emotional Self. The client in sorrow can visit joy; the passive client can locate aggressive instincts; and the depressed client can touch points of anxiety and excitement. Moreover, it is not only the obvious emotions and instincts which can be perceived as cyclical. Many attitudes and dispositions can be located in a convex and concave interchange. For example, introversion and extroversion; protectiveness and exposure; giving and receiving; certainty and vulnerability.

The next movement exploration which I have developed as an integral part of the Voice Movement Therapy methodology, and which I will now describe, allows the client to use the interchange between convex and concave body shapes to physicalise and amplify the interchange between emotions, instincts and attitudes which mirror each other.

Practical Method: Building the Convex and Concave Architecture

To begin, the client stands comfortably with their arms hanging loosely by their sides, breathing evenly through the mouth.

Photograph 2.1

Photograph 2.2

The client imagines that they are standing in the centre of the floor of Spherical Space. Clients then walk forward, experiencing the fact that with each step forward they also ascend, for the concave nature of the floor rises up before them. As the client moves forwards and upwards, they follow the natural tendency to arch back, creating a vertical convex curve at the front of the torso and a vertical concave arch at the back. Simultaneously, they then open out their arms to create a horizontal convex curve across the front of the chest and a horizontal concave arch across the back. Then, they imagine that they lean forward and rest into the concave wall of the sphere whilst simultaneously imagining that they stretch both vertically and horizontally across the convex surface of a sphere which sits behind them. Clients are now in the extreme forwardly convex position (Photograph 2.1).

Next, clients move backwards, imagining that they also move downwards, relocating themselves in the centre of the sphere, allowing the arms to drop once again to the sides. Then, clients move backwards, again imagining that they also move upwards due to the rising of the concave floor of the sphere behind them. As they move, they follow the natural tendency to arch vertically in the opposite direction, making a vertical convex arch with the back and a vertical concave arch with the front of the torso. They also, again, allow the arms to spread out to the side, producing a convex horizontal stretch across the back and a concave horizontal stretch at the front. Then, they lean back as though resting into the concave wall of the sphere behind them and simultaneously stretch over and lean onto the convex surface of an imaginary sphere which sits in front of them. Clients are now in the extreme forwardly concave position (Photograph 2.2).

Clients now find a rhythm and flow with which to move back and forth between these two positions, exploring the Convex and Concave Architecture. As they do this, they will begin to feel sensations of muscular stretching as well as sensations of an opening across and around the torso. The specific area around which these sensations constellate is the point just below the sternum; for this is in fact the centre of the Convex and Concave curve as the torso moves back and forth. When the front of the body moves into convex, it feels as though the impulse of explosion emanates from this point and that the curve has the centre of its crescent here. When the front of the body becomes concave, it feels as though the implosion emanates from this point and that the curve has the centre of its crescent here. As clients move back and forth between extreme Convex and Concave, they are encouraged to focus on their breathing and imagine that the breath passes in through the mouth and down a tube which fills the torso with air.

Now clients have experienced the convex and concave interchange in a forwards and backwards direction, they explore the same interchange moving from side to side. They step to the right, experiencing the simultaneous rising. Then they curve over creating a convex curve down the right side of the body and a concave curve down the left side. They raise the right arm and pass it over their head, extending the stretch. Then they imagine that they lean their right side into the concave wall of the sphere whilst simultaneously leaning onto and stretching over the convex surface of a sphere which sits to their left. Then, clients step back and down to the centre of the sphere before moving to the left side of the sphere where they create an extended convex curve with their left side and a concave curve with

Photograph 2.3

their right, passing their left arm over their head to extend the stretch (Photograph 2.3). Again, clients are asked to focus attention on their breathing imagining that the breath passes in through the mouth and down a tube which fills their torso with air.

Clients now have four points of a compass: front, back, left and right, and they now begin moving through these points, experiencing the ebb and flow of interchange within the Convex and Concave Architecture. In particular, they are encouraged to focus on the way that, as one surface of the body becomes increasingly convex, so its opposite surface becomes increasingly concave and vice versa.

The next stage of this exploration involves introducing the vertical dimension of convex and concave movement. Clients are now asked to discover ways of travelling up and down and across the concave floor and concave ceiling of their sphere, passing through concave and convex body shapes (Photograph 2.4). Because the imaginal floor of the sphere is concave, it cradles the body's convex surfaces and as clients begin to explore these

Photograph 2.4

movements, many will make infant-like gestures and experience child-like sensations (Photograph 2.5).

Clients move up and down, finding ways of contacting the floor, turning and rolling, coming back up to standing again. The client looks for surfaces of the body which present an opportunity for a convex and concave interchange, feeling the undulating ripple of semi-spherical movements.

Now clients have the basic Convex and Concave Architecture and movements in Spherical Space, they can take some time to personalise and diversify their creative movement. Clients are given time to move through Spherical Space travelling forward and back, side to side and up and down, focusing their attention on the interchange between convex and concave curves across different surfaces of their body. Again, clients are encouraged to breathe in and out through their mouth imagining that the breath passes through a tube which fills the torso with air. Clients are invited to re-explore Spherical Space allowing the convex curves of the body to lean into and be received and supported by the imagined concave surfaces of the sphere. This

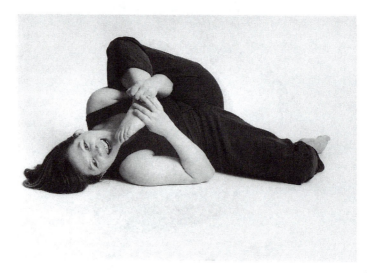

Photograph 2.5

soon turns naturally into a dance as the convex head, shoulders, abdomen, hips and other protruding body surfaces are cradled by the imaginal inner concave surfaces of the sphere (Figure 2.4). Meanwhile, the concave indentations of the body are imagined to be supported by convex surfaces of Spherical Space.

It is during this dance through Spherical Space that it is useful to point out again that while clients exaggerate a convex protrusion which is supported by the inner surface of the sphere, they are also inevitably creating an increased concave geometry on the opposite surface. In order to prevent these resulting concaves from causing vertebral compression or undue muscular fatigue, the client is asked to imagine that the grand sphere in which they move is populated with a variety of differently sized spheres, which fit snugly into all the concave spherical indents made by the body. For example, as the arms stretch up, the hips drop down and the left side of the torso creates a convex curve, resting into the concave wall of the grand sphere, so meanwhile the concave implosion created on the right side of the torso rests over the imagined convex surface of a sphere which gives further support. As the back protrudes and the spine curves over making a convex arch which leans against the concave wall of the grand sphere, the concave curve simultaneously made at the front of the body lies over the imagined convex surface of another sphere. As the head leans over to the right, clients conceive of a small sphere fitting snugly into the concave curve running down the side of the face and across the shoulder. In other words, everywhere there is a concave indentation created by the body, so it is imagined that this is supported by the convex surface of a sphere of equal magnitude (Figure 2.5). Meanwhile, the client moves so as to lean all convex surfaces into the receptive concave wall, floor and ceiling of the grand sphere which contains their movement.

Practical Method: Emotionalising the Convex and Concave

Clients now have the full architectural repertoire of basic movements with which to explore their emotional and psychological ebb and flow.

Returning to the instinctive and personalised movements through the Convex and Concave Architecture in Spherical Space, clients are asked to take familiar extreme emotions or attitudes and to locate them in particular body shapes. Then, as they move out of that body shape into its mirror opposite by turning convex surfaces into concave and by turning concave surfaces into convex, they seek to locate the opposite feeling or attitude.

Figure 2.4

Figure 2.5

Examples of common themes which clients have explored in my experience are:

Giving – Receiving
Angry – Frightened
Extroverted – Introverted
Nourishing – Exhausting
Depressed – Anxious
Defensive – Open

As clients begin to locate the interchange between mirrored emotions and attitudes in the physicality of the body's tendency to move through a Convex and Concave Architecture of shapes, they usually find themselves led by the process and a journey unfolds before them.

The following is an account of an exploration of Emotionalising the Convex and Concave Architecture in Spherical Space taken by Mary whom I introduced in Chapter 1.

Client's Account: Mary

Public Strength, Private Grace

I came into therapy for two main reasons. I was completely exhausted and wrung out and I had been having periods of extreme withdrawal, as though I was becoming a hermit. I had got to the point where I could not speak in public without shaking. This was unusual for me as I had always been a very outgoing person and managed people quite well. I was also fed up with feeling as though I did not matter and tired of spending my life looking after other people. I felt small and I wanted to grow big.

When I first starting moving through my Spherical Space using the Convex and Concave movements I noticed how I would thrust my body into convex curves quite quickly and hold myself quite stiff. Then I would collapse into a concave and feel quite exhausted, often falling to the floor. This physical pattern got me in touch with my emotional pattern of going from aggressive, driven and extrovert feelings and behaviour to an empty exhausted feeling. The thing that really struck me was that there seemed to be nothing in between.

My movements seemed very jerky and rhythmic and went very quickly from convex to concave. I started to realise that I was exploring two parts of myself. My public and my private Self. In my work I was quite 'thrusty' and assertive, dealing with lots of people. Yet, in my private life I was actually very shy and lonesome.

As I explored this separation between these two parts of myself through the Convex and Concave exercise, I noticed that whenever I moved into shapes that were concave at the front of my body, I covered my torso and my head with my arms. Yet whenever I was convex at the front of my body I kept my arms away as though exposing myself.

I associated being concave at the front with the feelings of quietude and exhaustion I have when alone. I associated the exposed convex shape with the feelings of strength and assertion I have in my public life, which has consisted mainly of caring for others.

I realised that I feel afraid of letting my concave side be seen. I keep a convex front and I keep my concave behind me.

As I journeyed through the dance, I began to realise how this must be exhausting me. In fact, after about five minutes I could not keep it up any more. It was too demanding and the rhythmic aggression of the dance was tiring me out. So, I started to slow the pace down and to let myself move from a convex front to a concave front very slowly. I also stopped covering my torso with my arms when I was concave at the front.

Because I knew the group leader was watching, and that others in the therapy group could see, I felt very exposed, as though someone had come in and seen me at my most private. Yet it was so easy, I felt I could go on moving and breathing for hours.

At one point, right in the middle of a transition between convex and concave, I began to cry uncontrollably. I felt as though a tight spot or a trap door which had been closed for so long had come bursting open.

Later, I volunteered to present my new-found concave movements and slow style of moving to the group. I wanted to see how it felt to move delicately and softly in public. When the group gave me feedback and used words like 'gentle', 'graceful' and 'kind' to describe my movement patterns, I could not help crying again.

I felt that I had cultivated an assertive and seemingly strong way of moving through the world. I had to appear strong and forthright because so many sick and weak people had depended upon me being there. Yet I had paid the price of having to keep my vulnerable side hidden. To have this side received positively made me wonder if I could afford to open up and let my delicate side and the side of me which needed to be taken care of be seen.

Practical Method: Sounding the Convex and Concave

The combination of focusing on the breath and locating intense feelings makes sound-making an inevitable next step in the exploration of Emotionalising the Convex and Concave. Many people, like Mary, find themselves weeping, sobbing, making audible breathing sounds or single note tones. The next stage of the work is to exaggerate and amplify these sounds and to observe how the tone and timbre of the voice changes as the body moves through convex and concave patterns.

Clients begin by returning to a standing position in the centre of the sphere. They breathe evenly imagining the breath to be entering a tube at the mouth and passing down into the torso. On the out breath, clients make a single tone, feeling the vibration of the sound echoing throughout the inside of the torso. Indeed, clients are asked to imagine that inside the torso there are echoing spheres (Figure 2.6).

Clients then begin to take a journey passing through convex and concave body shapes moving forward and back, side to side and up and down,

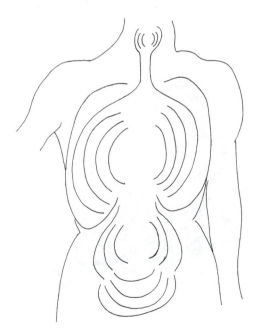

Figure 2.6

Photograph 2.6

Photograph 2.7

exploring the interchange between convex and concave surfaces of the body and locating specific emotional sensations in these movements. As they do this, they allow their voice to rise and descend in pitch, increase and decrease in loudness and change in timbre to give vocal expression to their emotional journey (Photograph 2.6).

The following is Martin's account of exploring Sounding the Convex and Concave in Spherical Space.

Client's Account: Martin

The Wheel of Fear and Anger

When we were asked to explore convex and concave movements combined with voice, focusing on a specific emotion, I chose fear without any hesitation. I had felt a lot of fearful emotions when originally establishing a Spherical Space and had felt the trembling in my voice and the sense of losing balance when I ventured away from the centre of my sphere.

The first sounds I made as I moved back and forth through convex and concave were very familiar to me. They were quiet and stuck in my throat with a kind of rhythmic spasm. But then I realised that I was not really moving into convex, I was mainly keeping concave at the front of my body and just sticking my chest out. So, I started to lead myself forward from the breast bone and make a convex arch.

I was stunned at what happened to my voice. The pitch dropped and it became very loud. I was really calling out, like a kind of war cry. As soon as I went back into the concave position the voice returned to its usual quiet rhythmic stuttering sound. So I went back and forth between concave and convex and between these two voices.

I started to experience the emotional changes very intensely. When in concave vocalising quietly I felt afraid, when in convex vocalising fully and loudly I felt full of anger. I kept going round and round like a wheel. Although the fear was extremely familiar to me, the anger was not. And yet, it felt very natural.

In the discussion afterwards I realised that I was carrying a lot of unexpressed anger: an anger that I kept hidden both from others and from myself. But it seemed to have come to the surface through the convex and concave work and I didn't want to ignore it.

Spherical Contact

Because our physique is spherical, it is most comfortably contained and supported by objects which mirror its convex or concave surfaces. The convex curves of the body's shape rest with ease in concave receptacles, like the buttocks in a well-worn indented chair seat or the convex spherical surfaces of the head lying in the concave indent of a pillow. By the same token, the concave implosions of the body receive comfortably convex spheres, like a tennis ball in the palm of the hand or the convex inner sole of a shoe in the concave arch of the foot.

This natural tendency of the body to fit with itself and with other objects according to spherical geometry is epitomised in the two primary developmental architectures: suckling and cradling. In suckling, the protruding convex nipple rests in the receiving concave sphere of the mouth. In cradling, the mother or primary care-giver creates a set of concave surfaces with arms, hands and torso which mirror, receive and contain the convex curves of the infant. As the baby's tiny body gyrates and wriggles, kicks and undulates, so the mother responds to the neonatal choreography with the kinetics of mirrored opposites, increasing degrees of concave receptivity where the baby's body becomes more convex and becoming more convex to fit snugly in the crevasses created where the baby's body becomes concave.

Photograph 2.8

The next stage of Spherical Space work, ideally suitable for group process, uses the symbiotic exchange of spherical choreography between mother and neonate as the foundation for an improvised dance called Relational Spherical Movement.

Practical Method: Relational Spherical Movement

With careful and methodical attention to one another's emotional state, two people bring isolated body parts together in a concave–convex relationship. For example, the spherical head rests in the concave curve of the partner's shoulder and neck. Then the partner becomes an initiator and bends forward creating a concave implosion of the torso which is supported by the other who creates a convex spine on all fours. This crouched position naturally creates a concave implosion of the abdomen and so the partner lying over the convex back now slides off and curls underneath, snugly fitting the torso into the abdominal concave.

As clients relax and increase their sense of trust, couples begin rolling over one another and a dance is created from the simplest and most archetypal somatic design, simultaneously listening for the rhythm and pattern of breathing and allowing the mechanical turn-taking to slip into a more fluid dance where it is possible for each partner to remain in constant contact with the other. By this process, the other's body begins to play the same role as the imaginary spheres in the earlier individual work. The other body becomes a womb and a cradle yet at the same time separate and distinct. In this work, each partner becomes a kind of substitute for the good mother who contains and cradles whilst at the same time, in alternation, each partner becomes the child contained by that mother (Photograph 2.7).

Practical Method: Sounding Relational Movement

The next stage involves both partners in continuing to dance in contact with one another, fitting convex and concave surfaces together as in cradling, but with the added dimension of vocalisation.

To begin, the two clients find a comfortable static position where they are cradled together. Then they focus on breathing in and out through the mouth imagining that the breath passes down a tube and into the torso and that the inside of the torso contains echoing spheres. They then begin toning on a single note feeling the sound resonate in their torso.

Then, slowly, they allow their voice to move up and down in pitch, to increase and decrease in loudness and to change in timbre, listening for periods of harmony and discord, sympathy and lack of sympathy. As they improvise the vocal duet, they allow their bodies to move, staying in contact all the time, so that a convex surface of one partner fits into the concave surface of the other and vice versa (Photograph 2.8).

Case Study: Mary and Martin

Taking Care and Giving Hell

When I asked the group to get into pairs to explore Sounding Relational Movement, Mary and Martin seemed to get together almost immediately. As the two began working together I was intrigued to experience the acoustic and physical dynamic between them.

At first, both seemed awkward and a little shy, but after a while they seemed to find a flow and danced in contact with one another as their voices blended together to make a sweet harmony. However, at one point, Martin curled up in Mary's lap. Almost immediately, Mary's voice changed from the light romantic tone she had established to a rough disrupted growling and her legs kicked from under her, forcing Martin to move.

Martin now moved around behind Mary and enveloped her back with his arms and legs, increasing the loudness of his voice and lowering the pitch in a seeming attempt to harmonise with her. However, Mary now settled back into the lighter voice as Martin rocked her slowly.

They reminded of me of two cats involved in a rapport that was at once playful yet aggressive, affectionate yet full of rivalry. This set of transitions between conflictual tension and collaborative concord seemed to provide the map for the rest of their work. This is Mary's account of her experience.

Client's Account: Mary

The Reluctant Nurse

In discussion afterwards I realised that in some ways it was typical for me to choose to work with Martin. Martin was someone in the group who was very clear that he wanted to be healed. His stammer was a great hindrance to him and he felt that if he could make it better he would have a new lease of life. Because of my history of always playing nurse, it was obvious that I would choose to work with him. However, as we began moving and vocalising together, I found myself actively and consciously avoiding getting into positions where I was holding him or making soothing sounds to him. As soon as I found myself in this position, my voice would get disrupted, loud and discordant with his and my body would wriggle itself to a new position where I could be held by him.

As we worked, I felt that our work was like a wrestling match, until about halfway through when I started to feel protected and nurtured by Martin. The problem was that I could not let myself enjoy it because I felt guilty that I did not want to care for him and uncomfortable that I sort of asked to be taken care of rather than it occurring naturally. So I was relieved to hear Martin's account of what we had done together.

But, when Martin started making his low loud sounds, I felt very solid and secure and when I opened my mouth, the high-pitched scream which I had wanted to make earlier during the Spherical Space exercise but had not been able to muster just came flooding out. However, because Martin sounded so musical, rather than just screaming, I seemed to be able to sing on and on really high. I felt like a diva.

The problem was that after what seemed like a relatively short period of time, I felt my throat clam up and the sound weakened. I felt that if I tried to go on any more, I would lose my voice – and this I found terribly frustrating.

Client's Account: Martin

Being Needed

As soon as we began moving and vocalising in contact with one another I could feel this incredible desire to look after Mary, as though she really needed to feel me. At first I felt worried because I seemed so big and clumsy and I did not want to smother her. Then when I got close to the front of her body and tried to rest in her lap, I could feel her pushing me away. I was glad. I only did that because I knew we were supposed to move in an exchange of convex and concave, taking turns to hold and be held. But when I felt Mary push me away I was relieved and my natural instinct was to go behind her and rock her.

The amazing thing was that as soon as I started holding and rocking her, my breathing relaxed and my voice felt and sounded smooth and without any restriction. As soon as I noticed this I began to realise that I rarely have any stutter or problem when I am alone with my children. I feel very protective towards my kids and it's as though their need for me is so strong that it overrides any blocks I may have. Mary sort of became my child and when the exercise finished I felt the kind of sorrow that I suppose parents must feel when their kids have grown up and don't need them in the same way anymore.

Because I felt this strong fatherly feeling, I returned to using the strong calling voice I had discovered earlier during the Sounding the Convex and Concave work. But whereas it had been like a kind of war cry when I first discovered it, now it was more protective, as though I was warding off any danger that might hurt Mary. When Mary then began to let out her high-pitched sound, it seemed to blend in with my voice to make a kind of strong wall around us that nobody could penetrate. It was an incredible feeling of protecting and at the same time being protected.

But, after a while, Mary's sound stopped, and in the quiet space this created I could hear that my voice was getting really tired and flimsy. This was really frustrating because inside I felt fired up and ready to go.

The Interface of Training and Therapy

When Martin discovered his strong calling voice and when Mary discovered her piercing scream, both of them became very excited and wanted to explore further those sounds and the emotions which they carried. It was as though the newly discovered extremity of vocal expression had enabled them to access a part of their emotional extremity which had hitherto been peripheralised. However, both Mary and Martin also felt frustration that their vocal instrument would not seem to give acoustic expression to the depth and breadth of what they felt; and they felt that they could only sustain the sounds which they had discovered for a short period of time.

The exercises and explorations which I have described so far do tend to animate the client's emotional sediment and bring implicit issues to the surface. And the most common experience which clients of all dispositions feel at this point is a frustration that their voice does not seem to be able to make the quality of sound or the quantity of sound which does justice to what they experience physically and psychologically. The vast majority of clients will describe their voice as feeling stuck, impeded, restricted, blocked and hindered.

This can be a frustrating place to be in the course of therapeutic work. For the psyche is alive and ready for growth, change and expression, yet the voice seems inadequate to represent it. In some forms of vocal work, the client is encouraged to express intense emotions through extreme sounds with little attention paid to building the strength and dexterity of the vocal instrument.

Although this may provide some short-term relief and sensation of discharge, it does not increase the capacity for the voice to give expression to a broader range of emotions over a prolonged period. In order for genuine therapeutic work to be done through a vocal medium, the voice must be trained and coached to increase in dexterity, strength and malleability.

Voice Movement Therapy may be compared to the other arts therapies. Whereas the drama therapist facilitates the expression of psychological material through drama, the dance therapist through dance and the music therapist through music – the Voice Movement Therapist focuses on the expression of psychological material through voice and movement.

However, because any kind of therapeutic Voicework involves expression through a broad range of sounds, many of which are unfamiliar to most people in their everyday discourse, the vocal instrument must be protected from misuse. Unlike the client of an art therapist, for example, whose instrument is the canvas or paper and brush or pen, the client of therapeutic Voicework is using a very delicate part of the body to express an extremity of images. Indeed, very often a client of any kind of deep therapeutic Voicework will give vocal form to the shadow, the darkest and most primitive aspects of the Self; and this delicate part of the body which is capable of expressing the shadow in sound is also highly susceptible to damage.

This is perhaps where Voice Movement Therapy is less comparable to the other arts therapies. For though the drama therapist, dance therapist and music therapist are facilitating the expression of intense feeling, they rarely offer tuition and training. Of course, in the other arts therapies it is perhaps less necessary, as physical damage to the person is less likely to occur. But in any vocally orientated psychotherapeutic practice the client is using a very delicate part of the tissue structure to express highly robust material. And unless the voice is trained to withstand such expression, the price of physical damage may be paid in return for psychological relief.

In order to attend to the need for vocal training, the next stage of Voice Movement Therapy involves direct work on the vocal instrument designed specifically to increase malleability and dexterity whilst protecting it from misuse. Central to this work is training the client to lengthen and expand the voice tube during vocalisation rather than submit to the usual tendency to constrict and shorten the vocal tract.

CHAPTER 3

The Voice Tube
Some Elementary Physical Principles
of the Vocal Instrument

The Physical Voice

The internal terrain of the human body is composed of an array of tubes or
cylinders: cylindrical or tubular veins and arteries which transport blood;
tubular intestines which transport digested food matter; tubular nerves which
transport neuro-chemical liquids.

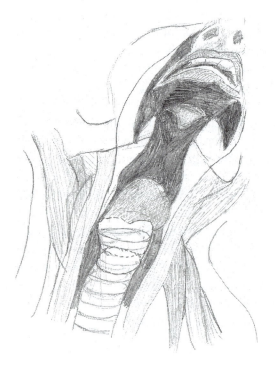

Figure 3.1

At various junctures, this complex network of cylinders distends and swells up into curved and curvilinear, semi-spherical organs such as the heart, the stomach and the womb. The result is an inner maze with outlets at the base and at the top of the body. The infant experiences the inner somatic landscape as such a set of tubes which connect with the outside world; and our early life is consumed with learning to control what enters in and what passes out of these tubes.

One of these tubes or cylinders of crucial importance to vocal expression is that which begins at the lips before branching into a labyrinth of conduits, ducts and channels which permeate into the lungs. When we breathe in, air passes in through the lips and along this continuous tube or cylinder, which for convenience may be divided into sections consisting of the mouth, the pharynx, the oro-pharynx, the larynx and the trachea (Figures 3.1). At the foot of the trachea in the centre of the chest this tract branches into two separate tubes known as the bronchi, each of which enters a lung (Figure 3.2). When we breathe out, air passes from the lungs and along the same passage in the opposite direction. This tubular passage of cylinders through which air passes is generally referred to as the respiratory tract.

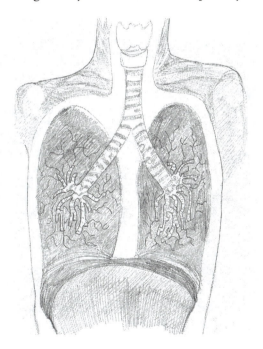

Figure 3.2

When we eat, the food substance which we ingest shares the same tube or passage as inspired and expired air for the first part of its journey, passing through mouth and pharynx, but taking a different route down through the oesophagus into the stomach. The direction of food away from the trachea and into the oesophagus and the direction of air away from the oesophagus into the trachea is controlled by a flap of tissue, called the epiglottis, which descends like a cover or trap door over the top of the trachea when we swallow food. The tubular passage of cylinders through which food substances pass towards the stomach is generally referred to as the digestive tract. The network of cylindrical pathways which further carry digested and semi-digested substances through the intestines of the abdominal cavity and expel faecal matter through the anal orifice is generally referred to as the gastrointestinal tract. Because both eating and breathing are core elementary experiences and processes, the first portions of this tube which host the passage of both breath and food is the locus for a pantheon of psychosomatic phenomenon. This is further compounded and intensified by the fact that vocal sound is also emitted through this tube in relation to which it is called the vocal tract or voice tube.

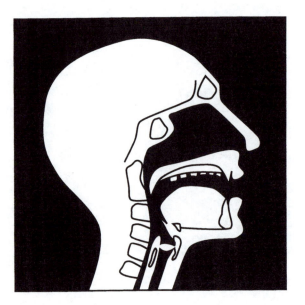

Figure 3.3

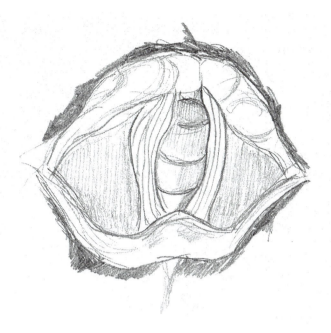

Figure 3.4

The vocal tract or voice tube begins at the lips, runs more or less horizontally to form the mouth, or oral cavity, curves downwards and narrows slightly to become the oro-pharynx, then curves to a further degree and opens out again forming the pharynx, at which point, if the head is facing forwards, the tube is now almost at right angles to where it begins at the lips. Then, the tube enlarges to become a cylindrical segment known as the larynx (Figure 3.3).

At the bottom of the voice tube, lying stretched out in the larynx, there are two folds of tissue called the vocal cords. At the front they are attached to the Adam's apple or thyroid cartilage and at the back they are connected to two movable cartilages called the arytenoids. The initial sound which emerges from the lips as a vocal signal is made by the vibration of these vocal cords.

The vocal cords are further attached to the trachea and the surrounding inner walls of the larynx by a complex set of muscles known collectively as the intrinsic laryngeal musculature. During normal breathing the vocal cords lie at rest, one each side of the larynx, like an open pair of curtains allowing air to pass freely through a window. The hole between the vocal cords

Figure 3.5

through which air passes is called the glottis (Figure 3.4). However, adjustments in the distribution of tension in the laryngeal musculature can cause the vocal cords to close, preventing air from entering or leaving the trachea, like a thick pair of curtains drawn tightly shut across a window (Figure 3.5).

The sound of the human voice is generated by the rapid and successive opening and closure of the vocal cords hundreds of times per second and it is to this process that people refer when they speak of the vibration of the vocal cords. The technical term for this vibration is 'phonation'.

This rapid vibration of the vocal cords causes the expelled air from the lungs to be released through the glottis in a series of infinitesimal puffs which create a wave which, between certain frequencies, or vibrational cycles, is heard as the sound of the human voice.

One of the criteria for a wave of air to be heard as an acoustic sound is that the constituting air puffs must be released at a rate of between approximately 20 per second and 20,000 per second. This means that the vocal cords must be opening and closing, or vibrating, between 20 and 20,000 times per second. Naturally, the ear can hear a wider range than the voice can sing, and the vocal cords cannot vibrate as slowly or as quickly as the extremes of this range. Singing the lowest note on the piano would require the vocal cords to vibrate about 32 times per second and singing the highest C on the piano would demand them to vibrate around 4,186 times per second; and there are not many singers who can do either. As a useful point of reference, singing middle C on the piano requires vocal cord vibration to be at a frequency of about 256 times per second.

Because the vocal cords are attached front and back to the thyroid and arytenoid cartilages, which are in turn connected to muscle tissue, they can be stretched out by tensile adjustment in the laryngeal musculature making them longer, thinner and more tense. When this happens, like all elastic objects which are tightened, they vibrate at a higher frequency producing a higher sound or pitch. Conversely, an alternative adjustment of the laryngeal musculature causes the vocal cords to slacken, so that they become shorter, thicker and more lax. When this happens, like all elastic objects which are relaxed, they vibrate at a lower frequency and the consequent sound of the voice deepens in pitch.

Whilst the speed at which the vocal cords vibrate determines the pitch, the force with which they hit each other during vibration determines the loudness. To make the vocal cords hit one another harder we have to increase the pressure of the breath travelling up from the lungs by employing the contractile power of the muscles of the chest and abdomen.

Pitch and loudness are therefore two of the acoustic ingredients or components which go to make up the sound of the human voice. In Voice Movement Therapy, the human voice is perceived as a composite of ten such fundamental components which combine to produce a spectrum of voice qualities and types. This system of component voice analysis is described briefly in Appendix 1 of this volume and is explained fully in my textbook *Therapeutic Voicework: Principles and Practice for the Use of Singing as a Therapy* (Newham 1997b). One of the most dominating of these components which contributes to the quality of the human voice is that known as 'harmonic timbre' which is the particular colour or quality which a voice has as a result of the shape and size of the voice tube.

Movement of the Tube

The voice tube or vocal tract runs from the lips, becomes the mouth, curls down to become the oro-pharynx, the pharynx and then opens out to become the larynx. And it is the shape and movement of this tube which governs so much of the specific quality of a voice which we hear, regardless of the note or pitch. Because of the laws of acoustics, the same note produced by the vibration of the vocal cords will resonate with a very different quality if the voice tube is short and narrow from the quality produced when the voice tube is lengthened and dilated.

To understand how the movement and configuration of this tube affects vocal quality it will be useful to imagine three crude tubes, closed at the bottom but open at the top, all made of exactly the same substance but constructed to different diameters and different lengths. The first is short and narrow; the second is relatively longer and wider; and the third is much longer and more dilated again. Imagine that we hold a tuning fork vibrating at 256 times per second – which produces middle C – over the top of each tube in turn and listen to the sound of the note echoing or resonating inside the tubes. In moving from listening to the sound inside the first tube to the same note echoing or resonating in the second and then the third, the listener would hear a change of timbre. Perhaps the sound in the first tube would sound 'bright', 'twangy', 'shiny' and 'shimmery'; perhaps the sound resonating in the second tube, by comparison, would sound 'thicker', more 'solemn' or 'fruitier'; and perhaps the sound resonating in the third tube would sound 'full', 'moaning', 'rounded' and 'dark'. Probably, the first tube would sound more comparable to a flute, the second tube would sound more comparable to the clarinet, whilst the sound produced by the third tube would sound more akin to the saxophone; they would all however sound the note C.

With regard to voice production, both the length and the diameter of the voice tube or vocal tract can alter, producing a variety of timbres, yet the pitch can be held constant by an unchanging frequency of vocal cord vibration. So, imagine that instead of a tuning fork at the top of three crude tubes, you have vibrating vocal cords at the bottom of one tube which can change its length and diameter to assume the relative dimensions of all three tubes. This gives some idea of how different timbres are created by the vocal instrument (Figure 3.6).

The vocal tract which runs from the lips down to the larynx is an elastic tube which can be increased or decreased in size by three options. We can expand the walls outwards, lower the floor downwards or raise the top upwards. In the case of the vocal tract, the lips mark the top of the tube, the vocal folds in the larynx meanwhile form the floor, whilst the roof and sides

Figure 3.6

of the mouth along with the curved surfaces of oro-pharynx, pharynx and larynx form the tubular walls.

The part of the tract where movement of increasing and decreasing diameter can be felt most easily is of course the mouth, which can open wide as in a yawn and close down to very narrow dimensions, as in whistling. But this opening and closing or sphinctral changes in the diameter of the mouth mirror the potential movements along the entire length of the vocal tract as well as within the larynx itself. In fact, if we allow ourselves to yawn fully, the complete length of the vocal tract including the larynx dilates. Conversely, this tract can be made to constrict.

The vocal tract can also lengthen and shorten. The first means of achieving this is to protrude and retrieve the lips and jaw, making the resonating tube longer and shorter respectively. The second means of achieving this is to lower and raise the floor by causing the larynx to descend and ascend in the neck. If you place your finger and thumb around your Adam's apple and yawn you may feel your larynx naturally descend in the neck. If you now stop yawning and whistle, you will probably feel it rise. As the vocal tract is that tube which runs from the lips to the larynx, the descending of the larynx in the neck actually makes the vocal resonating tube longer while the rising of the larynx in the neck makes it shorter, increasing and decreasing its length respectively.

Three Vocal Timbres – Flute, Clarinet and Saxophone

In place of the three crude tubes, we can now therefore pinpoint three arbitrary degrees of dilation and lengthening along the path of the vocal tract. The first compares to a flute-like tube, whereby the larynx is high in the neck and the tract is quite constricted, creating a short, narrow tube, such as when we blow a kiss or whistle. The second configuration compares to the clarinet-like tube, whereby the larynx is positioned in the middle of the neck and the tube is more dilated, such as when we steam up a pair of glasses. The third configuration compares to the saxophone-like tube, whereby the larynx is fully descended in the neck and the tube is dilated to its maximum, such as when we yawn.

If the vibratory frequency of the vocal cords is maintained at a constant, say at 256 times per second, producing middle C, whilst the vocal tract moves from Flute Configuration through Clarinet to Saxophone Configuration, the effect will be to sing the same note with three very distinct timbres, comparable to that achieved when playing the note C on a tuning fork held above the three separate crude tubes imagined earlier.

In Voice Movement Therapy, we give the vocal timbre produced by a short narrow voice tube the instrumental name 'Flute Timbre'; we name the vocal timbre produced by a medium length and diameter tube 'Clarinet Timbre'; and we call the vocal timbre produced by a fully lengthened and dilated voice tube 'Saxophone Timbre'.

In fact, the lengthening of the vocal tract by lowering the larynx also tends to increase the diameter of the tube, that is to dilate it. This operates according to the same principle as a collapsing telescope. When the larynx descends, it pulls the tissue walls of the pharynx down with it, reducing the thickness of the pharyngeal wall, causing the pharyngeal space to dilate (Figure 3.7). Conversely, to shorten the vocal tract by raising the larynx causes a simultaneous narrowing or decrease in diameter of the tract because when the larynx rises, the tissue of the pharyngeal wall piles up and thickens.

According to the acoustical laws which I have described, these alterations in length and diameter of the vocal tract have the effect of changing the

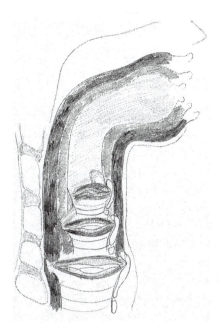

Figure 3.7

timbre of the voice. It is important to remember that the configurations of Flute, Clarinet and Saxophone are arbitrary and extreme positions of the vocal tract which, obviously, can form an infinite variation of combined lengths and diameters. The aim of the three timbres is not to imply a limitation but to offer distinct sensate positions and articulations against which the infinite possibilities of vocal timbral expression can be measured, experienced and adapted.

In order for clients to draw upon a malleable and dexterous voice which can give expression to a broad range of emotions without causing physiological damage, it is essential that the voice tube can achieve the flexibility with which to lengthen and dilate. For the movements of the tube create the acoustic diversity of sound which is needed to express a diversity of psychological experience. The problematic is that the muscular movements which lengthen and dilate the tube are so subtle that most clients find it hard to sense them and control them. In addition, working with the voice tube divorced from the whole body and separated from emotional experience is an empty and uninspiring task.

Therefore, in order to assist clients in developing the malleability of the tube and to help them achieve the three timbres, it is necessary to ground the vocal exploration in a somatic and psychological process.

Infant Instincts

The newly born infant experiences one of its first and most primary instincts in the stomach; and its hunger is expressed through the emission of sound through the mouth. The baby feels an emptiness, a hollow yearning for nourishment and it is this instinct to feed which rises up from the belly and out through the voice tube in the form of a hunger cry, an imploring for food. Because our first and most frequently experienced instinct is located in the stomach, many of the subsequent instinctual feelings which we host are localised in the abdomen. We tend to place our hand on our belly when we are in grief, when we are in shock, when we are consumed with laughter and when we are awash with sorrow.

The primary expression of deep instinctual feelings is vocal: cries, wails, moans, chuckles, guffaws, sobs and yells carry our anger, grief, joy and fear from the inner world of our psychic experience to the outer world of communication, where sound echoes our feelings in the ears of those who hear.

Because of the intimate connection between instinctual feelings and vocal sounds, it can often feel that the voice is like a continuous tube which runs from the lips down to the belly and through which our gut instincts rise up and emerge from the mouth. This experience is compounded by our early infantile sensations when the feeling of hunger in the belly and the sounds for hunger expressed through the mouth were simultaneous and conjoined.

For the baby, there is a greater sense of a continuous tube running through the centre of the torso, because, prior to conditioning, there is little taboo surrounding what goes in and what comes out of the tube. For the young infant, food is suckled at the lips and passes down the tube into the stomach. But it is also just as likely to re-emerge as regurgitated liquid as it is to be expelled from the anal opening at the other end of the body. Regurgitating food is natural for the baby and is not pathologised by the mother; in fact it is often a consequence of the rubbing of the baby's back to release wind. However, in time, the infant realises that once food has passed into the body through the mouth and down the tube, it should only exit again at the opposite end. From the point when this has been recognised, a re-emission of food from the mouth is then identified as a sign of pathology: we are only sick when we are ill.

As adults, it is easy for us to understand that there are really two tubes: one for breath and one for food. In fact, the first portion of these tubes are the same: the mouth and throat serve to carry breath and food. It is not until the tube reaches the depths of the throat that it splits into two: one journeying to the lungs and one journeying to the stomach. But for the infant, it just feels as though there is a hole in the face and a hole in the buttocks and that the two holes are at opposite ends of a tube.

The preverbal infant uses the voice to express instinctual feelings and is not yet ready to articulate sounds to communicate thought. However, in time, the instinct to articulate is born and the instinctive sounds of crying, cooing and babbling lead into the formation of the first words which give expression to the formation of the first thoughts.

As thought and language develop, the child begins to locate the act of thinking in the head. Indeed, most adults naturally localise the experience of thinking in their head. We touch our brow when in deep thought, but rarely when we are in deep feeling. Whereas instinctual feelings seem to rise up from the belly to emerge from the mouth as sounds, thoughts seem to descend from the head to emerge from the mouth as words. Both feelings and thoughts, then, have to pass through the throat where they feel as though they are converted to sound. This makes the throat a kind of bottleneck, a point of convergence between the two major pathways: the pathway of thoughts which descend from the head and the pathway of feelings which arise from the depths.

Many people choose to work therapeutically through voice because their issues connect to a conflict between thought and feeling and their voice feels impeded by ambivalence and confusion regarding what they should express, vocalise, regurgitate and expel and what they should retain, silence, stomach and digest.

In Voice Movement Therapy, people often feel that when they dilate and open the vocal tract to Saxophone Configuration, they contact physical and emotional sensations which seem to be located in the abdomen. When they close the voice tube to Flute Configuration, the sensations subside. This is primarily because most people do not dilate and lengthen the vocal tract to the dimensions of Saxophone Configuration unless they are vomiting or in deep sobbing. Although clients want to expand the voice tube and allow their guttural feelings to be vocalised there is also often a fear that they will regurgitate food. This causes ambivalence and conflict and the client will often fight against the expanding voice tube dimensions, succumbing to the tendency for the muscles to contract and constrict the tube.

The next stage of the work involves providing the client with a fluid physical and vocal paradigm that will facilitate expanded vocal tract dimensions without conflict, constriction or fear. This next stage, which I shall now describe, also enables the client to explore the interface between thought and feeling and to locate the two ideokinetic centres of expression – the head and the belly – connecting them to the two voice timbres of Flute and Saxophone respectively.

Practical Method: Head Voice – Belly Voice

To begin, clients imagine that the impulse to vocalise originates in their head and that the sound gives expression to their thoughts. Standing comfortably with arms hanging loosely by their sides, clients breathe in and out, making the smallest possible tube with their mouth and throat, narrowing it to its minimum dimensions – as though breathing through a straw. They try to imagine that the voice tube begins at the lips and travels through the mouth, around into the throat and then stops at the little indent between the clavicles at the base of the neck. This makes the breathing quite shallow and because the tube is so narrow, the rate of breathing tends to speed up in order to inspire sufficient air. Clients then begin to tone on a single note feeling that the sound resonates in the head and they are encouraged to focus on their thoughts. This produces the Flute Timbre voice.

Now, whilst continuing to vocalise, clients open and lengthen their voice tube to its maximum dimensions, as we do naturally when we yawn. They now imagine that the tube extends from the lips all the way down into the belly. And they now imagine that the instinct or impulse to vocalise originates in the belly and that the voice resonates throughout the abdomen. This produces the Saxophone Timbre voice.

Clients then go back and forth between the head-based Flute Timbre voice and the belly-based Saxophone Timbre voice by changing the dimensions of their voice tube and alternating the imagined impulse for vocalisation and seat of resonance between head and abdomen.

The problem with such a sudden transition from very short and narrow dimensions to maximum dilation and lengthening of the voice tube is that it recapitulates the action of vomiting. It is, however, important that the client experiences this radical transition and is offered an opportunity to explore the fears surrounding the 'bringing up' of material. For, underneath the fear of vomiting is the psychological fear of expelling psychological material that is 'sick'. Indeed, many clients of Voice Movement Therapy have to face the fact that giving vocal expression to the true Self involves making sounds which represent the dark side of the psyche through voices which are often heard as ugly.

This exercise also highlights the radical distance that exists between the thoughts of the head and the instinctual feelings of the belly; and many clients experience a conflict between the two. One part of the Self wants to expand the voice tube and produce the rich resonance of the Saxophone Timbre, vocalising deep feelings. Meanwhile, another part of the Self wants to close down the voice tube and remain within the safety of the shallow Flute Timbre voice, perfect for articulating words.

Practical Method: Heart Voice

Between the seemingly emotionless thoughts of the head and the deep instinctual feelings of the belly there is an intermediary place: the heart.

The emotions which we tend to locate in the heart are of a different order to those which we place in the belly. We tend to associate the heart with love and courage, with the sentiments of romance and the source of sympathy. The belly, meanwhile, seems to host our fear, our grief and our most guttural joy. The next stage in this practical method gives clients an opportunity to find this third area of vocal and emotional expression: the heart.

Standing with hands loosely by the sides, clients again breathe in and out through the mouth holding the voice tube in its minimum dimensions, as though breathing through a straw. They begin vocalising with the Flute Timbre imagining that the impulse to give voice and the place of resonance is the head. Then, they open the tube so that it is wider than in the Flute Configuration or head voice but not as wide as in the Saxophone Configuration or belly voice. They then imagine that the tube begins at the lips and carries on down into the middle of the chest, ending at the place just below the sternum which provided the central physical impulse in the Convex and Concave work. This produces the heart-based Clarinet Timbre voice. Clients now alternate between these three physically localised voice placements, going from head, to heart to belly. As they do this, they imagine that their voice gives expression to their thoughts, their heart-felt emotions and their gut instincts respectively. Clients then go round in a cycle from head to heart to belly to heart to head, feeling the emotional transitions and listening to the changes in vocal qualities from Flute Timbre through Clarinet Timbre to Saxophone Timbre which accompany changes in the voice tube dimensions.

The Psychology of the Open Throat

Learning to expand the vocal tract is not just a physical pursuit with acoustic results. It is a psychological process with deep emotional implications.

The voice tube, particularly the throat, is a highly charged part of the body. Neurologically it is one of the most highly innervated areas of the body; that is to say it is served by a vast circuit of nerves. Psychologically, it is at the core of so many psychological issues: issues of expulsion and retention, issues of extroversion and introversion, issues of penetration, issues of speaking up and of being silenced, issues connected to eating and digestion and issues which go to the heart of what it means to have or not have a voice and therefore a place in the world.

Because of the highly charged nature of working with the voice tube, working with physical exercises which are aimed at encouraging vocal tract expansion tends to stimulate complex psychosomatic reactions which need to be handled with sensitivity, accuracy, compassion and care.

The following are accounts by clients of this work, beginning with Mary and Martin, whose journey has already been established in the previous chapters.

Client's Account: Mary

The Recoil to Safety

So far, during vocalisation in Voice Movement Therapy, I had been experiencing the breathiness of my voice. I had also been consistently hitting a wall or a ceiling which prevented my voice from getting higher and louder.

However, during the process of trying to lengthen and expand the voice tube, I began to hear and feel the difference between Flute and Clarinet. I realised that my normal voice was stuck in Flute. When I managed to produce Clarinet for the first time, I was astonished at how easy it was to raise the pitch and increase the loudness, and the sense of a block, a wall or ceiling seemed much less. My voice went up and down, loud and quiet and I felt a sense of power and strength.

The problem was, I could not get the voice tube to expand into Saxophone. Every time I felt it open a little, it sort of recoiled back or else my throat seemed to cramp up and the sound would become choked. I would then return to my comfortable Flute voice for fear of losing sound altogether.

Client's Account: Martin

Trouble with the Tube

I could not open the voice tube beyond Flute. It is as simple as that. When I did start to feel an expansion in the back of my throat I just coughed and gagged and felt as though I was going to be sick. At one point, I quite violently stretched my throat open and tried to imagine the tube lengthening all the way down into my stomach, but I felt so nauseous and I started to retch. I had to leave the room and go to the toilet to open my bowels.

When I tried again, I realised that, though I wanted to find the Saxophone voice, I was also quite frightened of going on. I felt as though if I did manage to open the voice tube, the contents of my stomach would come rushing out.

I also noticed how movement in the voice tube gave me sensations running up into my head. When I managed to briefly open and lengthen the voice tube, it seemed to release pressure in my head, almost as though I was letting off steam from my head through my mouth. Then, when my voice tube narrowed, as is normal for me, I had the sensation of pressure building up in my head again.

Client's Account: Janice

Fear of Opening

I came into therapy a few years after I had been raped, suffering from a number of physical symptoms including a lot of restriction around my voice. Since the rape my throat had felt like a lump of metal and I felt like I had a metal bar running down my chest.

When I was vocalising in Flute, I could produce a clear tone within a pitch range of about just over an octave. When I expanded my vocal tract to Clarinet, it became easier for me to sing with more volume and the range increased by about half an octave. But when I tried to expand the voice tube to Saxophone my muscles seemed to tense and I started gagging. I also seemed to get a little breathless and my voice weakened as its range decreased to about an octave. I tried to fight against this, emptying my lungs with as much force as I could, expecting an enormous sound to come rushing out, but the more I tried, the weaker my voice became and the more helpless I felt.

On comparing my sounds to those of other people in the group, I realised that I had not managed to expand the voice tube even to a full Clarinet.

During my work towards trying to open the tube, I felt I understood what was happening. Since the rape I had, obviously, felt that I needed to keep everything closed, from my vagina to my mouth. When you have been abused like that, penetrated so violently in such an intimate place, you just want to close all your open places.

My throat had just closed up as a protective instinct, but I was paying the price of silence. I knew that in time I would be able to open my tube into Saxophone, but I would have to reclaim the feeling that it is safe to be vulnerable.

Client's Account: Ian

The Belly of God

I am a church leader and spend a lot of time speaking and singing at the head of the congregation. Yet I know that my voice is restricted. I came into therapy to see if I could loosen my voice but also because of some inner conflict between my spiritual convictions and my own emotions. I feel an increasing struggle with myself as more and more of the feelings which possess me seem negative and destructive. There have been times when I have felt hypocritical, speaking to members of our church about *their* negative feelings, knowing that I have these feelings as much, if not more, than they do.

Vocalising in Flute was obviously easy for me and I found I could create my own kind of plainsong chant, both high and low in pitch. It took me a while to manage to open the voice tube to Clarinet and when I did, the voice which emerged was a stranger to me. It sounded more masculine, richer and a lot more emotionalised. I found myself wanting to sing a blues song – but I did not know any so I made up a kind of jazzy improvisation. Then, after a prolonged attempt, I managed to expand my vocal tract fully and produce the Saxophone Timbre. This shocked me. My Saxophone voice was like nothing I could have imagined myself producing. It sounded crude, loud and booming. I found myself stomping about the room singing like a drunkard and feeling the vibrations resonate throughout my body.

I must say that a part of me felt a little frightened; for it felt that a hundred years of emotions and a great pantheon of characters were rushing out of my soul – as though a trap door had been opened and they were all taking an opportunity to escape. One thing I knew for certain was that this voice was the place I needed to explore – the emotional voice which knew no reason yet seemed to be a part of me. I hoped that I would in time be able to use this voice to serve God.

Overcoming the Rigid Tube

Many people who attempt to produce the three vocal timbres of Flute, Clarinet and Saxophone find it impossible at first to fully dilate and lengthen the vocal tract. At the first attempts, some do not manage to get further than Flute, some manage Clarinet and only a few can produce Saxophone. There are many psychophysical reasons for this and the next stage of Voice Movement Therapy is to provide exercises and processes of exploration that enable clients to produce the three timbres and benefit from the ability to draw upon a malleable and dexterous vocal tract.

Because the voice tube is embedded in the terrain of muscles which weave a loom throughout the entire bodily frame, achieving vocal dexterity necessitates working with the whole body rather than with only the fine movements which control the larynx. Furthermore, because working with the three harmonic timbres provokes deep psychophysical reactions, it is extremely grounding to have magnanimous physical movements and postures in which to locate specific psychological material. The throat is so tiny that, without body work, it can feel as if the entirety of one's psychological experience is condensed into this tiny area and the client can feel a sensory overload in the throat.

The next process of investigation which is core to the methodology of Voice Movement Therapy and which I will describe in the next chapter therefore aims to locate the highly significant movements of the voice tube in the motion of the entire body.

CHAPTER 4

Cycles of Sound and Movement
Structured Voice and Movement Techniques for Exploring the Self Beyond Words

The Tube, the Body and the Voice

The voice tube is the most important part of the body when it comes to combining voice and movement. It is like a conduit through which the inner world of imagination and emotion passes out. And it is primarily lack of malleability in the muscles which lengthen and dilate the tube which causes restricted and impeded vocal expression. In this chapter I will describe a series of three movement explorations which are designed to enable clients to achieve voice tube malleability, locating the three primary voice timbres of Flute, Clarinet and Saxophone. But, the practical methods which I shall describe in this chapter are simultaneously designed to enable clients to explore three distinct levels of psychological material: the personal, the archetypal and the spiritual. The methods comprise three physical and acoustic explorations called Developmental Postural Cycles which are a series of vocal sounds, postures and movements:

Cycle 1: The Personal Developmental Postural Cycle

Cycle 2: The Instinctual Developmental Postural Cycle

Cycle 3: The Spiritual Developmental Postural Cycle

Vocal Development in the Infant

It is the sound of the voice which marks the birth of every healthy neonate and in days of old, if babies did not cry out on arrival, they were induced to do so by the proverbial slap on the posterior. The life and soul of the baby depends upon its capacity to breathe and the voice consists of nothing but this breath made audible by the puffs of air rhythmically released by the vibrational opening and closing of the vocal cords.

Within moments of being born, the mucus clears from the baby's throat and soon after, it cries. This cry of birth is the first mark which a human being makes upon the world. Moreover, healthy neonates will compose melodic structures of rising and descending pitch using the full vocal range available to them from the moment they are born.

At 14 days old a baby's vocal folds are only about 3mm long and the lungs are so small that he or she has to breathe at a rate of around 90 cycles per minute in order to inspire sufficient oxygen to remain alive. But despite the size of its tiny body the baby is able to make an incredible volume of sound by maintaining a very high pressure of air from the lungs against the vocal folds. Sometimes the baby sustains this intense sound-making for periods of such duration that it continues to amaze scientists that damage resulting from misuse of the laryngeal apparatus in neonates is almost unheard of.

For the first three months, the baby cries only as an expression of hunger and distress, the melody of which rises and falls like a siren. To midwives and paediatricians worldwide, each of these new-born cries is much like any other; however, within weeks a mother will be able to distinguish her child's cry from that of many others without face-to-face contact. The mother has an innate aptitude, an inbuilt ability to detect the idiosyncratic cadences, the unique quality of rhythm and melody which her baby alone possesses. In addition to these tonal cries the baby also makes what are called vegetative sounds: coughs, dribbles, hiccups, lip-smacking, burps and wheezes which result from physiological processes. It is this orchestra of vegetative sound, so instinctive and necessary to the infant, that is rarely tolerated in adults within many cultures.

Many clients coming to work on their voice have a very fixed idea of the vocal sounds which are acceptable and those which are not. For many, the idea of making vegetative primitive sounds of little etiquette are abhorrent. Yet it is so necessary that such acoustic prejudices be overcome and that the voice be permitted to give free reign to the complete canvas of potential emissions, as it is in early infancy, if the original and primal malleability of the voice is to be rescued from the constriction of social priority.

At around three months old a new quality of crying emerges which also has a rising and falling melody but which usually has a slightly higher pitch range than the melody of distress. This is identified as the emergence of the first pleasure cry. We observe this basic developmental acoustic principle as adults when pleasurable experiences instigate an instinctive rise in the pitch of the voice. From the emergence of the so-called pleasure cry, the mother is able to differentiate between cries of hunger and cries of tiredness, between cries of physical discomfort and those of emotional irritability, between cries of distress and those of pleasure. In short, the mother has the capacity to perceive in the infant's melodic arrangement of pitch a language which is as sophisticated as the baby's needs.

The emerging pleasure sounds contain acoustic properties which act as the precursor for the vowels that will later be used in words; and the differentiation between the melody of distress and that of pleasure is the baby's first step towards the acquisition of speech. However, whereas the verbal infant will later organise such sounds according to the rules of the dictionary, the baby, not yet familiar with such a scheme, arranges them according to an intuitive, creative and innate sense of pitch, melody and rhythm in a fashion akin to the composition of music. This instinctive musical arrangement of spontaneous vocal sounds in which are recognisable the raw material for vowels, is known as 'cooing'.

Between the ages of about three and six months a new kind of sound called 'babbling' issues forth. Babbling is identified as the emergence of sounds which form the raw material for consonants. The first to occur are those known as 'back consonants' in which the air flow from the larynx is interrupted at the rear of the oral cavity, such as 'k' and 'g'. This is followed by the production of what are called 'labial consonants' in which the air flow is interrupted at the front of the mouth, such as 'b' and 'm'. The ultimate achievement of the babbling stage is the ability to combine these new staccato percussive sounds, which are akin to consonants, with the earlier sustained tonal sounds, which are like vowels. This gives rise to a stage in the child's communicative development which rewards parents, researchers, linguists and paediatricians with the utmost pleasure and fascination. The child talks in its own language in which the attentive listener can hear, or so she thinks, words from her own language, words from foreign languages, and words which are pure ingenious invention. This babbling continues until around 12 months by which time the vocal folds in a healthy infant will have developed from their original 3mm to around 5.5mm; these continue to grow and by 15 years old they are about 9.5 mm. Simultaneously the original rapid rate of breathing slows down as the lungs grow in size.

Up to about 12 months, the acoustic utterances of the baby – the crying, cooing and babbling – emerge purely instinctively and not as a result of any instruction from the mother or care-giver. Deaf babies cry, coo and babble just as hearing babies do. The vocalisation is phylogenetically inherited in the same way as the instinct to suckle at the breast; it is one of the biological patterns of behaviour which the human species universally possesses; and despite the unique quality to each baby's voice, there is a ubiquitous similarity to the crying, cooing and babbling of all babies that is recognisable worldwide. It is these innate universal qualities that give it a specific quality of humanity and which may be described as the universal acoustics of primal vocalisation.

Artistically speaking, prior to the acquisition of language, the solo improvising dancer emerges from the womb to become her own accompanying vocalist, weaving the original and eternal song and dance routine that celebrates life without need for translator, director, conductor or choreographer. It is during this stage, before the rules of speech have been demanded of the infant, that the rudiments of songful composition and performance are explored, which are often impeded by the overwhelming demands of language.

Many adults who experience vocal constriction do so because of a residual restriction left over from the difficulty of passing from non-verbal to verbal expression as an infant. To acquire language, the infant must gain a precise control of the vocal musculature, bringing sounds under the obedience of a strict code of linguistic signification. There is a great pressure upon the child to get this right and those children who appear slow or impeded in their ability to master language are often singled out for special attention at the behest of worried parents. The main task which the infant faces is to narrow the voice tube so that it is constricted enough to articulate the fine vowels and consonants. The price paid for this essential transition is that it then becomes very difficult for the adult to return to the expanded dilated dimensions of the voice tube which the preverbal infant possesses. Although narrow voice tube dimensions are perfect for articulation, they do not serve liberated non-verbal vocal expression which requires expanded voice tube dimensions in order to achieve a broad resonant harmonic spectrum.

For adults who still feel uncomfortable with language and who feel that their voice tube is narrowed and constricted, the first cycle, called the Personal Developmental Postural Cycle, provides an opportunity to revisit the early experience of passing from non-verbal to verbal vocalisation. Through this process, some of the infantile anxieties surrounding the period of language acquisition can be revisited and resolved. In addition, expanded voice tube dimensions can be reclaimed.

Practical Method: The Personal Developmental Postural Cycle

The first of the series of cycles in Voice Movement Therapy, then, is the Personal Developmental Postural Cycle.

To begin, clients stand erect with arms hanging loosely by the sides of the torso, with the vocal tract shortened and narrowed into Flute Configuration and with the lips, tongue and jaw held as though ready to speak. From this posture, clients move around Spherical Space in what I have called Walking Position (Figure 4.1). As they move, they allow the voice to ascend and descend in pitch, to increase and decrease in loudness and to create spontaneous semi-articulate sounds with teeth, lips, tongue and jaw. Clients are asked to amplify the tonus in the muscles around the vocal tract and to focus on a thoughtful head-based impulse to vocalise. As they move and vocalise they are encouraged to allow actual words, preferably words of their mother tongue, to emerge and be precisely articulated.

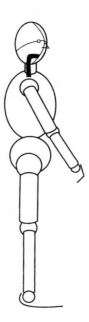

Figure 4.1

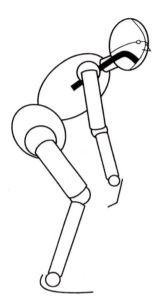

Figure 4.2

Second, clients allow the legs to bend at the knees, the torso to implode into a concave curve at the front, the pelvis to tilt forward and descend towards the floor and the head to hang over so that the eyes are focused downwards. This mirrors the concave curl of the foetus. As clients move into what I have called the Squatting Position (Figure 4.2) they travel around their Spherical Space and allow the vocal tract to open and lengthen as they step back from articulate sounds and words and begin to babble, creating a kaleidoscope of sound comparable to that which the infant makes during the babbling stage, using the heart-based Clarinet Timbre voice.

Third, clients fall forwards, place the hands on the floor before them, bring their knees into contact with the ground and assume the Crawling Position (Figure 4.3). As they do this they allow the vocal tract to fully dilate and lengthen, as though belching, yawning or regurgitating. As they do this they are asked to imagine that they have taken a step further back in their development to a stage when they were completely inarticulate, producing crying and cooing sounds using the belly-based Saxophone Timbre voice. Clients then roll over onto their sides into a fetal position, onto their back and through onto all fours and into the Crawling Position again, before coming up through the Squatting Position into the Walking Position with simultaneous shortening and constricting of the vocal tract.

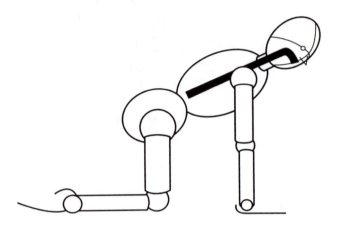

Figure 4.3

Clients then begin the cycle again, personalising the choreography and orchestration, allowing the notion of a child-like exploration to infuse their acoustic and kinetic expressions, passing from Walking Position, allowing the body to descend downwards, giving in to the pull of gravity into Squatting Position; and continuing down to explore the Crawling Position on the floor.

This choreographic journey provides a framework within which to experience a degree of regression to an infantile form of movement and vocal tract behaviour. As clients become familiar with the cycle, they begin travelling through Spherical Space, walking, crawling, squatting, moving themselves around from each of the three positions. Through this process, clients experience the degree of muscular tension which is required to hold the vocal tract in Flute Configuration in preparation for speech and begin to relinquish such necessity, focusing on the acquisition of expanded vocal tract dimensions which will later serve increased non-verbal vocal malleability of expression.

First Steps

From the moment of birth, the infant moves; and mobility occupies a central place in the child's development. For the newly born baby, walking is a long way off indeed. Walking is the culmination of months of experimentation and there are stages which must be passed through in order to achieve the ability to walk. Most importantly, the way that the infant passes through these stages – the kind of support which she gets, the kinds of responses she receives for her achievements, the amount of time the baby is allowed to experiment with movement uninterrupted, the degree to which the environment is safe for such experiments to be pursued – all these factors make up the foundations upon which the baby learns to walk.

Some babies are suddenly snatched up by an anxious mother the moment they get too near a potentially dangerous object. Some babies are left for hours in a play-pen where the maximum space afforded them within which to practice mobility is a few feet. Some babies have to crawl around on cold floors. Other babies have an environment of safety, encouragement and support.

The amount of room we have to move physically as infants influences how much room we feel we have to move and develop psychologically. By retracing the footsteps of our early physical movements, we can bring to the surface sensory memories of our early mobility and relate them to the way we move physically and psychologically as adults.

Because the voice is the primary means by which the preverbal infant expresses his feelings, vocalising during the exploration of early movement patterns in adult therapy tends to bring to the surface the deep feelings which a person has regarding the degree to which they feel free to move – psychologically and physically. By combining movement with sound, deep historical feelings and sensations originating from early experiences can be uncovered and related to the present adult Self, providing an opportunity for growth and transformation.

Case Study: Martin

A Case of Gagging and Stammering

To recap, Martin was 36; he was married with two children and had driven a taxi for 12 years. His reason for attending work with me was that he had what he described as a 'stutter' which no previous endeavour had succeeded in alleviating. He found it difficult to remember exactly when he developed a 'stutter', but he felt that it was around the age of eight. I noticed at first that his 'stutter' was irregular and vowels were as equally affected as consonants. However, the most striking thing about Martin's speech pattern was the involuntary jerking movements of his head and neck which accompanied vocalisation and which were particularly exaggerated during his 'stuttering'. His eyes closed, the head tilted backwards and to one side, the neck stiffened and his facial muscles contorted. His head would then jerk rhythmically and spasmodically for the duration of the interrupted sound. The look upon his face during such episodes was, to my personal eyes, one of tremendous fear. Then, on further listening to the so-called 'stuttered' sounds, I noticed that in fact, what was happening was more adequately described as a kind of contorted gagging of the larynx. The sounds which occurred during this balking were in Flute Timbre and sounded strained and contracted; and he described that it felt as though 'air could not get out'. I therefore became convinced that the majority of Martin's speech difficulties originated not in what would be clinically described as a 'stammer', which causes a 'trip over words', but in a constriction of the pharynx and larynx. The amount of times he stumbled over consonants made with tongue or lips were actually very few, but the gagging occurred with all vowels as well as with certain consonants, particularly 'k', during which he would extend the sound into a gurgling noise which, if I refrained from witnessing the fearful expression on Martin's face, reminded me of a baby regurgitating or expelling unwanted milk.

Martin could not locate any single incident in his life which he could describe as severely traumatic. However, he spoke about his relationship to his father as having been a source of ongoing trauma. His father was a devout and extremely strict Catholic and a professor of chemistry; his other two sons were both doctors. It had been clear from quite an early age that Martin was not going to reveal the same predisposition to academic activity as the rest of his family. Another significant memory for Martin was that he had been the brunt of jokes made by his peers at school and by his brothers at home, who called him 'bunny' because he had an involuntary twitch in his cheek. And, though Martin could not locate any single traumatic event, it became obvious over the period of our work together that his entire childhood had been a very unhappy one. Not only did he grow up in the shadow of his brothers' achievements, but he also had a mother who showed him little attention and no physical affection. He could not remember ever being held or cuddled or kissed by his mother; furthermore, he never saw his parents hold hands or show any physical signs of love to one another. The picture of his family life that emerged was an incredibly sterile one. Dry academic conversations, competitive brothers, meals at regular times often with guests who would parade their expert intellectual preoccupations, and a mother with a cool and distant relationship to her sons and her husband.

When I first met Martin I had asked if he had any other illnesses or difficulties apart from what he described as his 'stutter'. Martin had replied that he had for many years suffered periodically from extreme headaches. He dealt with them by taking a variety of analgesics but they rarely alleviated what he described as the 'sensation of pressure between his temples'. On investigating further the genesis of these headaches, it was revealed that they worsened during times of extended verbal activity; the more he 'stuttered' the more his head ached.

Martin liked his job as a taxi driver because 'on a bad day' he could 'get away' without talking to anyone. However, on a good day he would enjoy chatting to his customers and was frustrated intensely because he felt the 'stutter' was preventing him from partaking of the social activities which he enjoyed. Martin was also keen to point out that as a taxi driver he frequently escorted customers of some importance – 'scientists', 'writers', 'actors' and others whom he described as having 'made it'. When asked to describe how he thought such people perceived him when he 'stuttered', Martin was categorical that he appeared 'stupid'. The words he used to describe the way he thought that he was perceived included 'daft', 'idiotic', 'a moron' and a 'dim-wit'. It emerged that these were all words which his brothers had used against him.

It also emerged gradually that Martin had associated verbal proficiency with intelligence. The fact that he had not 'lived up' to the academic standing of his father and brothers had made him feel stupid and his voice problem further compounded this feeling and in many ways became a symbol for it. It was also clear that Martin wanted sympathy for his condition, and indeed he responded very eagerly to a sympathetic attitude. In this respect he had very clear memories of his grandmother. She had been a very important figure in his life as a child and a single source of comfort, understanding and physical affection; she had also been very kind about his 'stutter'. It was also his grandmother who had told him that when he was born the doctors had told his mother that he was 'much too small and light' and that she should rectify this by feeding him twelve bottles of milk per day. Martin had therefore been awakened from sleep continually as an infant and had been force-fed with milk.

As I asked Martin to articulate different sounds and listened to his gagging, I could not help but see him still as a helpless baby being force-fed, desperately trying to spit out unwanted milk, screaming and crying and not knowing whether to swallow or spew. On asking Martin to speak of his defecating habits he admitted that he suffered from both constipation and diarrhoea and rarely had prolonged periods of normal bowel activity. With this information in mind, I heard in Martin's vocalisations the strained, contracted sounds which we all make when trying to defecate during constipated periods.

I therefore asked Martin to extend all the sounds on which his pharynx constricted and simulate the sounds of a baby being forced to swallow milk which in fact it wishes to expel. Naturally, this provoked some resistance in the form of embarrassment and irritability; however, with gentle persistence he began to compose a very authentic symphony of baby-like babbling sounds made up entirely of the noises which arose from his inability to speak. The entire vocalisation was produced with the vocal tract in Flute Configuration and I found the quality of the sound moved me to tears which stimulated in me a desire to rescue him.

As I listened to him vocalise, I noticed that he had his hands clasped together and that his voice, when I listened through a musician's ears, had a quality which reminded me of a Gregorian chant. It had lots of free air and was very quiet in a middle pitch range. I asked Martin to exaggerate the posture and the voice by raising his hands as in prayer and focusing imaginatively on the image of a monk. Though this was easy for Martin, it also caused him some resistance because my suggestion reminded him of the religious demands of his father.

I knew that Martin would only overcome his gagging if he could vocalise with expanded voice tube dimensions and so I began to encourage him to open and lengthen the vocal tract. I asked him to stay with the monk image, but to imagine the figure to be fatter with a protruding abdomen and encouraged him to allow the vocal tract to lengthen and dilate into Saxophone Configuration. Although Martin was able to make progress with this, he became extremely agitated at this work, expressing fear and worry about 'what might come out' if he 'opened it all up'. He described feeling insecure when his 'throat expanded' as though he was going to vomit and not be able to 'control the spillage'. He also said that the work was beginning to cause him to be flatulent. I therefore began to teach Martin the Personal Developmental Cycle, enabling him to pass from the constricted Flute Configuration and Flute Timbre of the Standing Position through more dilated and lengthened dimensions of the vocal tract, working towards the Saxophone Configuration and Saxophone Timbre in the Crawling Position.

The act of crawling and vocalising became very appealing to Martin, as he crouched on all fours and cooed and spat, opening the pharynx to resonate a gentle sound yet one rich in harmonic resonance. As his voice discovered the Saxophone Timbre, we realised that he had a beautiful bass voice and that he could sing the most complex linguistic phrases with complete fluidity, not stammering or gagging on a single sound. At one point during the exploration, Martin made a quality of sound which was more raucous than I had heard from him before; and he sat on the floor and placed his hands on his head explaining that he felt a 'weird sensation' going from his temples down through to his anus.

As Martin practised the vocal and physical work over a period of time, he reported two developments: firstly, his defecating habits normalised and secondly the frequency of his headaches substantially reduced.

It seemed that Martin's infancy had been couched in some confusion with regard to what should come out and what should stay in. Firstly, he was forced to take in more milk than he desired and his natural instinct to expel it had been quashed by a mother who had been told to force it into him. Secondly, his parents had placed great pressure on all of the children to 'express' or 'push out' intelligent language and 'digest', swallow or keep in anything that was not the material for academic progression. Martin, in realising he was not as 'bright' or as 'clever' as his siblings had therefore kept quiet and when he did say something was simultaneously aware that it would not be welcomed or received with any respect or affirmation. Martin's thoughts and words were, like his milk had been, all stored up inside him desperate to get out yet forced to stay in. This had led to a build-up of pressure, causing headaches and constipation which frequently transformed into unstoppable diarrhoea when he could not hold any more inside him. When we began working through the Personal Developmental Cycle, his fear was that the equivalent to diarrhoea would come flowing uncontrollably out of his mouth in the form of 'shitty sounds'. So the constriction of the vocal tract served to prevent this from happening.

Indeed, when we did dilate and lengthen the vocal tract, Martin experienced a feeling of endless fluidity, with the bass and baritone quality of his voice flowing like a deep dark river. In fact, the first song we worked on with this newly discovered voice was *Ol' Man River*. But in time, Martin was able to shape and sculpture this voice in speaking and singing, articulating language without any gagging or stammering and without the ambivalent feelings of fear which originated in an infantile confusion about what should be taken in and what should be expressed.

Practical Method: The Instinctual Developmental Postural Cycle

The second of the three cycles is called the Instinctual Developmental Postural Cycle and is a variation on the kinetic cycle of postures and movements which I named as the Personal Developmental Postural Cycle above. Its purpose, like the purpose of the Personal Developmental Postural Cycle, is to provide a system of physical, respiratory and vocal exercises which enables the client to achieve maximum malleability of vocal expression by learning to control the lengthening and shortening, dilation and constriction of the vocal tract. The Instinctual Cycle, like the Personal Cycle, also assists the client in finding the three distinct elementary vocal timbres of Flute, Clarinet and Saxophone by grounding these deeply in the body and its movement. But most importantly, it provides an opportunity to access and explore instinctual and archetypal impulses which exist beyond the realm of personal history.

During this work, attention is again drawn to the lengthening of the vocal tract whereby the drop of the larynx vertically in the neck is used as the basis for an ideokinetic image of the tube of vocal resonance extending further down the body. By this method, the natural movement of the larynx in the neck is amplified to create the imaginary picture of the vocal tract actually lengthening down the entire torso. Simultaneously, as the voice tube is lengthened, so it is also dilated.

The first stage by which clients enter this process involves shortening and dilating the vocal tract to its Flute Configuration and vocalising on different vowels within a comfortable pitch range. The physical position during this is similar to that which in personal developmental work I have called Walking Position. The client stands erect with straight legs and arms hanging by the sides, with a concentrated expression of the physiognomy and the eyes focused on a particular object in space. The client imagines the length of the tube to run from the lips down to the concave indent between the clavicle at the base of the neck. This posture and its accompanying Flute Timbre voice is called Homo Erectus.

The concentrated facial expression is a highly important part of the Homo Erectus for a number of reasons. Firstly, the narrowing and shortening of the vocal tract during the articulation of language demands tensile activity of the physiognomical muscles which form facial expression. Speaking therefore influences facial appearance by physiological necessity. Secondly, speaking serves to articulate thought by sculpturing cognitive conceptual information into acoustic segments. The concentrated expression of the face in the Homo Erectus posture helps to compound and amplify the experience of such a relationship between thoughtful activity and narrow vocal tract dimensions. As the client vocalises in Homo Erectus, the impulse for vocal expression and the seat of resonance is imagined to be in the head, further relating the Flute Timbre voice with the realm of thought.

From the Homo Erectus, the client is enabled to enter into the second posture which in personal developmental work I have called Squatting Position and which in the Instinctual Developmental Postural Cycle is further developed into what I have called Primate Position. Here, the legs bend slightly at the knees, the pelvis tilts forwards, the space under the arms increases, the physiognomy relaxes, the eyes lose specific focus and relax into peripheral vision where the entire optical span is given equal attention, the jaw drops passively, as in the excessive salivation during drooling, the oro-pharynx and pharyngeal space falls open into passive dilation, the larynx descends in the neck and the vocal tract moves from Flute to Clarinet Configuration with an accompanying shift in acoustic quality. As clients drop down into Primate Position they are encouraged to imagine the tube lengthening so that it now extends down to the bottom of the sternum. Simultaneously, clients imagine a shift in the impulse to vocalise from the head to the heart. In moving from Homo Erectus to Primate, there is an initial feeling of a drop in the centre of experience from the head to the chest, as though in Homo Erectus one is focused on the articulation of the thoughts which abound in the mind; whilst in Primate there is a letting go of this sensation and an awareness of the moods and sentiments of the heart. So, in Primate Position, clients imagine that the emotions of the heart are being expressed through the voice and that the seat of resonance is the chest.

Central to the effective use of this posture to facilitate vocal tract expansion is the willingness of clients to give up conscious cognitive concentration as they drop down into the Primate Position. Because the predominance of thought in the mind tends to prepare the mouth for the articulation of that thought through language by causing a narrowing of the vocal tract, it is difficult to let go of the necessity of such preparation whilst thought predominates. Clients are therefore required to allow an expression of bland, vacant emptiness to cover the face as the muscles around the forehead, jaw and cheeks relax. To mirror the relaxation of the thought process further, the eyes stare out into infinite space, letting go of directed vision as the mind releases itself from directed thought.

As the client physically drops down into Primate Position, they notice the sensation of a deeper, fuller stream of breath. They also hear a radical change of vocal timbre which sounds resonant with more harmonic content. To assist in the achievement of a discernment between the Flute and Clarinet timbres, clients are enabled to return to Homo Erectus, experiencing the gradual contraction and shortening of the vocal tract as the legs straighten, the space under the arms closes, the eyes refocus on a specific object, the face resumes its expression of cognitive concentration and a predominance of thought returns. The client then moves back and forth between the two positions of Homo Erectus and Primate, experiencing a regression to a preverbal mode of functioning expressed physically through the ape-like postural position and acoustically through an inarticulate but resonant vocal expression.

When clients have successfully managed to allow a genuine dilation and lengthening of the complete vocal tract into the Clarinet Configuration, the next stage is to attempt to allow the vocal tract to dilate and lengthen to its maximum potential during vocalisation, producing the quality of voice referred to as Saxophone Timbre. To assist with this the client moves into a third animal position known as Feline-canine which is similar to that which I have named Crawling Position in relation to personal developmental work.

Whilst the animal image for the Primate Position is the great ape, here the client imagines a combination of lion and wolf. From Primate Position, the pelvis tips completely, the arms fall towards the floor, the legs bend from the knees, the body moves into being supported on all fours, the head raises, the vocal tract actively dilates to its maximum diameter, the larynx descends further in the neck and the voice expressed is fully resonant. As clients drop down into the Feline-canine position, they imagine that the tube extends from the lips all the way down into the abdomen, as though the lungs have dropped into the belly. The client now imagines that the impulse to vocalise comes from the instincts and gut feelings of the belly and that the seat of resonance is the abdomen as they vocalise in the Saxophone Timbre voice. In fact, as the client drops into Feline-canine, the entire gravitational relationship of the body to the world shifts, and the belly which has hitherto been held vertical to the ground now falls horizontal to the earth with the organs hanging down off the spine. The belly is now the under-belly. In Feline-canine, there is therefore a sense of the centre of experience dropping down into the gut emotions of the lower regions.

The quality of the consequent Saxophone Timbre voice is imaginatively comparable to the baying and howling of a wolf and the stretched soporific sounds of the great cat; it is also similar to the sounds produced when one sings and yawns simultaneously and those produced during deep and prolonged sobbing.

The drop from Primate into Feline-canine represents a further regression from the semi-articulate acoustics of the great ape to the completely inarticulate expressions of the wild cat and dog. Indeed, because in Saxophone the vocal tract is so expanded, the articulation of consonants as well as the production of distinctive vowels is barely possible.

To further enable the discernment between the three distinctive timbres, the client can now pass back from the Feline-canine position through Primate and return to Homo Erectus before journeying again regressively down through Primate into Feline-canine. The client repeats this descent and ascent whilst the practitioner meanwhile assists and supports, guides and instructs until the client is able to expand and contract, lengthen and shorten the vocal tract by their own volition, producing an ever more distinctive vocalisation of three elementary timbres.

Clients then begin the cycle again, personalising the choreography and orchestration, allowing the notion of animal instincts to infuse their acoustic and kinetic expressions, passing from Homo Erectus, allowing the body to descend downwards, giving in to the pull of gravity and moving into Primate Position; and continuing down to explore the Feline-canine Position on the floor. The client now has three distinct bodily positions correlating with three animal images which utilise three distinct vocal tract dimensions.

Primal Archetypal Regression

On one level, the Instinctual Developmental Postural Cycle is simply a pedagogic technique to enable clients to expand vocal tract dimensions. However, needless to say, the work presents the client with challenges which invariably provoke highly affective responses. Therefore, it is necessary to understand that beneath the pedagogic layer of the methodology is another dimension which instigates a therapeutic process.

Working with the Instinctual Developmental Postural Cycle tends to instigate what I have called Primal Archetypal Regression. Whereas the Personal Developmental Postural Cycle tends to recapitulate early sensations and experiences originating in the specific personal infant history of the client, working with the Instinctual Developmental Postural Cycle tends to animate deep archetypal sensations and feelings originating in the collective unconscious.

In Primal Archetypal Regression, clients use the Instinctual Developmental Postural Cycle as a springboard from which to explore a menagerie of animal movements and sounds, shifting the tendency for regressive activity, which non-verbal vocal expression inevitably inspires, into a transpersonal framework. In Primal Archetypal Regression the tendency towards personal regression to infantile vocalisation is located in an archetypal regression to an animalistic form of vocalisation. In other words, rather than expressive regression to personal infancy, there is an expressive regression to human primitivism.

Clients begin standing in Spherical Space, vocalising with little effort. The practitioner then verbally guides the clients through the Homo Erectus, Primate and Feline-canine movements, encouraging them to vocalise with the distinctive qualities of Flute, Clarinet and Saxophone. The client is then encouraged to diversify the repertoire of animal essences, using the body and the voice to personify a menagerie of real and imaginary creatures.

Animals represent core archetypal fantasies within the collective unconscious; the ape, the lion, the wolf and the bird, for example, represent human potentialities in a network of legends, myths and parables worldwide. The werewolf, for example, is an image which has occupied a dominant place in the collective psyche from Paleolithic animal cults to the myths of ancient Egypt, from European societies to Hindu cultures. The primitive and underdeveloped human Self is mirrored in stories of human beings, particularly men, turning into wolves and more frequently women turning into cats; no less proliferous are the myths of the human that can transform into a flying bird. Moreover, one of the most frequently recurring motifs in the dreams of all peoples is the animal; and there is not an adult alive who has not at some time dreamt of wild creatures, both real and imaginary. These animal constructs, therefore, go to the heart of the imaginative collective unconscious and assist the client in paving the way for an exploration of the deeper strata of the psyche through sound and movement.

As clients move through the animal positions, they develop a kinetic choreography which emulates the great cat, the great dog and the great ape and a host of other creatures which resonate with the clients. Through careful guided instruction, clients are enabled to personalise their own mythic creature and develop an acoustic pattern and physical choreography through which they personify animal essences. As clients enter into this process, the sounds become wild, unformed, savage and primal and the vocal tract instinctively lengthens and dilates.

Throughout the guided journey, the practitioner continually intervenes with containing instructions and eventually brings the session to an end, creating a period of silence in which clients can return to a sense of conscious cognition.

In utilising this work I am attempting an acoustic and somatic realisation of Jung's concept of an archetypal human shadow, that part of the human which is still primitive, savage and little separated from the animal. Jung believed that the lowest levels of the shadow are indistinguishable from the instinctuality of the animal, reminding us of a time when the distinction between humanity and animality was not so great (Jung 1953, pp.233–234). All of the dark, chthonic and downward pointing aspects of ourselves converge in the collective unconscious as the archetypal shadow. The more society demands that humanity should be ordered, tamed, controlled, passive and civilised the more the human shadow tends to become chaotic, savage, wild, ferocious and primitive. Primal Archetypal Regression asks the client not only to shed language and enter into the primality of non-verbal vocalisation but also, by implication, to shed the developed and matured social and psychological graces, mannerisms and constructs which language is adept at describing and enter into the spirit of pure instinct.

A minor acknowledgement of the psyche's animality and instinctuality is perceivable in common English language usage where animal metaphors provide a vivid representation of qualities integral to our human nature: sly as a fox, cunning as a shrew, stubborn as a mule, slow as a snail, dog tired, strong as an ox, beavering away, slippery fish, dirty rat, filthy pup, lion-hearted, lone wolf, dark horse, stupid ass, fly like an eagle, feeling sluggish, frightened as a rabbit. Many of these metaphoric usages, however, are not employed to openly express one's own animality but to berate, belittle or degrade the person to whom such a metaphor is applied. Such use is made of animal metaphors to degrade women who are variously described as bitches, cows, dragons and pussies and nowhere was an image more heinously employed than in Nazi propaganda where Jews were portrayed as rats to further disseminate the anti-Semitic comparison between the Jewish race and vermin to be exterminated. Such demeaning projections remind us that consciousness actively seeks to avoid identifying with the shadow and therefore the beasts. Primal Archetypal Regression provides an opportunity to overcome this conscious resistance by appealing to our propensity for animal empathy, which is perhaps exemplified most vividly in the myth of Tarzan, who could communicate with animals (Farmer 1972). The idea that humans share the same language as animals is also epitomised in the story of Dr Doolittle (Lofting 1950), and brought somewhat closer to reality in the testimony of Dian Fossey (1983) who liaised with the *Gorillas in the Mist*. By understanding the way that animals and non-speaking humans think, feel and experience their world, we hold up a mirror to an aspect of our own functioning.

Amongst the various speculations upon the elements which distinguish humans from the animals is the proposal that only human beings have cultivated a complex acoustic communicative code of language which is culturally specific and transculturally translatable. This code is distinct from the sounds made by other animals by our advanced ability to vary the acoustic signal made by the larynx with subtle articulations of the mouth, lips and jaw using incredible precision and dexterity. Consequently, language and the capacity to articulate is a predominant psychological symbol for conscious development. Conversely, therefore, inarticulate sound-making – the grunts, groans, screeches and calls of the voice unshaped by the speech apparatus – provide an acoustic reflection of psychological primitivism; and Primal Archetypal Regression provides a container and an expressive framework for such a process. To enter into a matrix of non-verbal vocalisation is therefore not only to reverse the developmental process on a personal level but also to entice the shadow-laden aspects of the collective unconscious forward into the arena of therapeutic investigation. This, naturally, leads to resistance. The more primitive vocal sounds heard in daily life, such as yawning and belching, lead us to literally place our hands over our mouth. This may, in part, be because these preverbal utterances remind us of the primal and untamed aspects of ourselves which, deep down, still growl like the bear, roar like the lion and screech like the hawk. If so, relocating the capacity for such vocal utterances provides a container for the exploration of the shadow; and nothing could be more therapeutically pertinent.

Case Study: Mary

To be Wild and to be a Mother

As I stated in Chapter 1, Mary was 52 when she first came to work on her voice. She was a woman of petite proportion and slim dimension who spoke gently and quietly and whose reason for attending was a tiresome irritation with frequently feeling 'small', 'quiet' and somewhat 'taken advantage of', describing her image of how people perceived her as 'a soft touch'. In addition, she suffered from an overwhelming shyness, a feeling of inferiority and what she described as a 'paralysing lack of confidence'. She had, in the past, suffered two periods of debilitating depression for which she had been prescribed anti-depressant medication.

Mary had not had the opportunity for formal education beyond her late teens, despite a deep interest in and aptitude for the sciences. When she was 15 her mother died and she was forced to look after her younger sister and brother. Shortly after her siblings had left home, her father had fallen ill with Parkinson's Disease and she had nursed him until he died.

During the period of nursing her father, she had met a man eight years her senior whom, after her father's death, she had married and with whom she had three children. During the taking of her case history, she told me that she had enjoyed motherhood and that she maintained a close relationship with her children. Shortly after her last child had left home, her husband became very ill with cancer and she nursed him for two years before he died. Since her husband's death, one year prior to our meeting, she felt 'completely at a loss'.

Mary had always wanted to sing but had been discouraged by her husband and her children due to her sounding 'out of tune' and had in addition felt it imprudent to spend money on singing lessons when the children already needed more than the family's financial resources could bear. Now, however, she had taken a job and had decided to explore her voice.

She had chosen to investigate her issues through Voicework because she felt that it was primarily through her voice, which she described as 'shaky', 'trembly' and 'thin', that her unassured personality was expressed; epitomising this, she said that during her depressive periods she had remained 'almost dumb'. She also said that she had been told that she was 'too quiet', 'too slow' and that her voice was 'monotonous' and 'difficult to listen to' by a number of people close to her.

As we began working with simple exercises involving Mary in the intoning of single notes ascending and descending the pitch scale, I noticed that, from the perspective of my own subjective counter-transference, her voice seemed aged and wise but seemed to lack any frivolity or youth. I asked Mary to try to imbue her voice with a quality of child-likeness. However, this was to no avail. We both agreed that her voice lacked a child-like spirit.

When we discussed her difficulty in finding the child's voice it became apparent that Mary felt that her childhood had been taken from her and that she had been untimely and prematurely propelled into adulthood by the death of her mother, when Mary was 15, upon which she was forced to assume adult duties before her time. She had raised her younger sister and brother almost single handed and buried deep beneath Mary's brave face of 'having come to terms with this' there was an 'anger and a resentment' which she felt she had put out of sight.

In a later session, after considerable analysis of the effect of her lost youth, I asked her to sing the highest note of her comfortable pitch range, imbuing it with an attitude of 'spiteful resentment'. When she did this, the sound became very loud and nasal and there emerged a voice more intense and emotive than I had heard her sing before.

I led Mary through the Instinctual Developmental Postural Cycle and within a short space of time, Mary was moving and vocalising, creating her own animal repertoire. At one point, she spanned her arms like wings and began making flying movements, spinning around and around accompanied by a high-pitched screeching sound. Over the next 20 minutes Mary composed an extravagant dance of her voice, rushing like a tornado up and down the pitch scale, singing and moving, creating a panoply of winged creatures. She became a hot-blooded prehistoric 'ravenasaurus', soaring at top speed across valley and plain, brandishing her beak and bellowing out the cries of hunger. She became a great winged compound, part heron and part stalk, perched and poised; she became a screeching pink flamingo, a squawking magpie, a wild black crow and a parrot with the full prism of plumage. As Mary journeyed through the matrix of bird imagery her voice became very loud and extremely powerful; and she became particularly engaged in the transformation back and forth between the stalk and the crow. The former she felt symbolised the role of nurse and midwife she had played all her life whilst the crow somehow stood for the 'blackness' and 'anger' which she felt.

During our analysis of the work, Mary spoke about her memories of the role of surrogate mother which she had played to her sister and brother and began to reveal her unexpressed resentment, not only towards her mother for dying but also towards her brother and sister for requiring care, her own children for 'taking every ounce of energy she had' and towards her husband for falling ill and leaving her 'unprovided for'.

During her description, Mary happened to say that her sister had always accused her of being spiteful and that she had in fact been quite malicious during her own childhood. Furthermore, after the death of her mother she had recurring dreams in which her sister died, releasing Mary from the burden of care-giving. In addition, during the mothering of her own children, she often had sporadic 'spiteful' feelings towards them and she often felt that they kept her from 'living her own life'. However, Mary had repressed all this because it was 'negative and destructive' and 'anyway' she said that she loved her children dearly.

As we continued working, I guided Mary through a process of Primal Archetypal Regression, encouraging her to embody animal images and essences which gave a framework within which to release and explore her sense of repressed spite and resentment.

As she passed down into Feline-canine position, her head dropped, her hands gripped tight and she held her posture with her sight line passing down her torso, as though looking through her legs. Then she began to cry.

The Feline-canine position had caused Mary to experience the weight of her breasts hanging from her chest and this physical sensation had somehow encapsulated and crystallised her feeling of having been 'sucked dry' by her brother, sister, children and husband leaving her 'shrivelled' and 'empty'.

I gave Mary the image of a drought-weary lioness, fatigued with heat, worn and exhausted with well-suckled nipples, prowling through the bush. She sang soporifically, with wide gaping yawns in Saxophone Timbre and with a very slow vibrato.

Then, as she explored the Feline-canine movements, she seemed to discover a fresh energetic quality with which she began to move and vocalise with complete engagement. She hissed and spat and clawed, her voice manifesting extremely fast vibrato as it passed back and forward between modal register and falsetto register. She concocted a liquid voice made of arsenic and strychnine and there emerged the character of a creature half cat and half crow, with an acidic voice which burns and bleaches with every note. Then, as she rolled over onto her back, she sang like a viper, like a boa constrictor. I asked her to decrease the loudness and make the spite more conniving and ensnaring, like a spider slowly and cautiously spinning a web of death and then as a scorpion quickly and impulsively injecting the poison. The images of insects increased both the quality of spite and the intensity and strength of the voice. Now as we worked, a fresh network of images unfolded in the voice which built up an emotional field composed of a premeditative revenge against an oppressor; and she became a character, half insect and half crow, with a fatal sting that aimed to kill, slowly.

Gradually, these emotions and images birthed a voice nearly one and a half octaves higher than when we had started and which sounded calm, strong and self-possessed.

The next time we worked together she manifested a voice which we both experienced as full of vitality, freshness, youth, energy and verve and she began to explore sounds associated with childhood. Her voice gurgled and effervesced with innocence and naïveté, she sang with the freshness and purity of a kitten untouched by trauma; and as she sang, Mary's face took on an open and inquisitive smile which I had not seen before.

The discovery and liberation of a more liberated and malleable voice had been, in Mary's case, connected to the release of spite, resentment and anger which also acted as a discharge of and an absolution from the bottled-up energy which its repression had caused. Meanwhile, the animal imagery of the Instinctual Developmental Postural Cycle and Primal Archetypal Regression had provided a framework within which Mary could explore the shadow side of the good nurse and the good mother, an entirely necessary process for someone who had been prematurely denied her own mother and forced into assuming the role of a good mother herself.

For Mary, to explore such issues could have been a terrifying process; and the use of animal imagery provided a means of distancing it from the personal, thereby offering a degree of safety. Furthermore, animal metaphors help the client to sense that, despite the magnitude of personal trauma, there is often a universal structure lodged beneath the personal narrative which reflects broader issues. In Mary's case, such issues were not composed only of elements of her own neuroses but were, in many respects, political factors arising from the way circumstances had made functional use of her at the expense of so much of her soul. Furthermore, her issues were connected to the age-old archetypal nature of the mother in all her aspects – nurturing and destroying, compassionate and spiteful, bitter and sweet.

Practical Method: The Spiritual Developmental Postural Cycle

The third cycle which completes the three Voice Movement Therapy Developmental Postural Cycles is called the Spiritual Developmental Postural Cycle and is aimed at helping the client in finding a sense of spiritual well-being. This cycle is modelled on the choreography and psychology of the prayer.

The notion of prayer is predicated on two primary elements: to ask and to give thanks; and these two conditions of being are not unique to Christians but permeate the nature of everyone's psychic disposition.

This prayerful construct is frequently evident in therapy where the client asks the therapist for help and when such requests are answered gives thanks and expresses gratitude. Of course, the client also experiences the frustration, rage and despair towards the therapist which Job expressed towards God upon the mountain.

The prayer is also a vocal form, like the lullaby and the ballad; and in all Voicework this artistic structure can provide a context for the expression of asking, the utterance of thanks at receiving and the release of negative

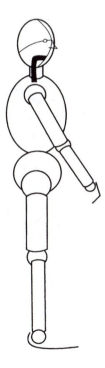

Figure 4.4

feelings in response to sensing that one's needs or prayers have not been answered.

The use of the prayer in Voice Movement Therapy is grounded in the matrix of positions and movements which I have called the Developmental Postural Cycles and which I have explained in relation to developmental work and in relation to an instinctual and archetypal exploration above. In this third cycle, a variation of these positions is explored in relation to the process of praying; I have called it the Spiritual Developmental Postural Cycle.

First, the client stands upright in what I have called the Walking Position in relation to developmental work and Homo Erectus position in relation to instinctual and archetypal work. In this position, the client explores choreographed movements of arms and hands which express the act of asking and receiving. As they do this, they vocalise with the head-based Flute Timbre voice timbre using narrow and shortened voice tube dimensions. As they move and vocalise, clients allow their voice to articulate in a spontaneous free-style semi-articulate language, as though prophesising. This is called the Standing Prayer (Figure 4.4). Second, the client allows the knees to bend and the torso to descend into the position which I have called

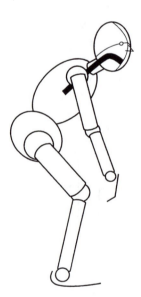

Figure 4.5

Squatting Position in developmental work and Primate Position in instinctual and archetypal work. Here, the client drops the head, tilts the pelvis forwards and allows the torso to implode into a Concave Architecture as though praying in a sitting position. Choreographing imploring movements with the arms, the clients allow voice tube dimensions to lengthen and dilate and they continue to vocalise with a spontaneous use of phonology, akin to speaking in tongues, using the heart-based Clarinet Timbre voice. This is called the Sitting Prayer (Figure 4.5). Third, the client drops down into what I have called the Crawling Position in developmental work and the Feline-canine position in instinctual and archetypal work. Here, the client bends down placing the hands and knees on the floor and explores the notion of praying on the knees. In this position, clients allow the voice tube to lengthen and dilate to its maximum dimensions and continue to sing in the belly-based Saxophone Timbre voice. This is called the Kneeling Prayer (Figure 4.6). Fourth, the client slides down onto the floor so that the entire body is stretched out facing downwards, as though praying prostrate as they continue to vocalise. This is called the Prostrate Prayer (Figure 4.7). The client then comes back up through the Kneeling Prayer and Sitting Prayer positions arriving at the Standing Prayer position. They then begin

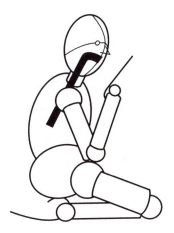

Figure 4.6

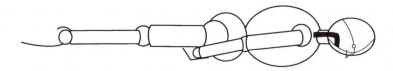

Figure 4.7

the cycle again, personalising the choreography and orchestration, allowing the notion of spiritual aspiration to infuse their acoustic and kinetic expressions, passing from the Standing Prayer, allowing the body to descend downwards into the Kneeling Prayer; continuing down to explore the Sitting Prayer; and on down to the floor to explore the Prostrate Prayer.

As clients proceed through this choreography, they continue to allow the voice to journey, discovering an original language without recourse to specific linguistic signification. Through this work, clients are enabled to contact the universal nature of need, want, receipt, thanks and frustration independent of specific transient contents, subjects or issues. Moreover, one of the inspiring aspects of this work is that, in the instinctual and archetypal work of Primal Archetypal Regression, the process of moving from Homo Erectus down to the floor serves to bring the client closer to the animality of the psyche and its tendency for primitive descent. The same downward movement in the prayer work, however, serves to bring the psyche closer to the core of its most spiritual aspiration. The work can therefore provide an opportunity to heal some of the split between the animal and spiritual within us.

Case Study: Jonathan

To Turkey in a Wheelchair

Jonathan was mentally handicapped, a term which descends from a terminological lineage which has included 'imbecile', 'stupid', 'retarded' and 'backward'. Jonathan had been in a residential home for 30 years and in that time, only the name used to describe his condition had changed. He was 38 years old, had deep green piercing eyes, gigantic teeth and hands like plates; and the first time I saw him he was sitting in a circle in the common room of his home with 37 men and women ranging in age from 22 to 61, who had gathered obediently to take part in a 'voice workshop'.

Jonathan had been classified 'non-verbal'; he had spent some time with a speech therapist in his early twenties but to no avail. Though he was non-verbal he was certainly highly vocal; his voice sporadically emitted a stream of guttural sounds accompanied by an undulating and wave-like dance of his arms, as though he was saying goodbye to a departing loved one knowing she would never be seen again. Jonathan had been abandoned at the age of six; his parents were still alive but had not visited him for 23 years. The staff at the centre thought his sporadic vocal emissions to be harmless but meaningless.

I was once travelling in Turkey during the festival of Ramadan. It was a hot and dusty evening and the town was deserted. As I turned a corner to buy some water, I heard a sound which grabbed my attention: a moaning, pleading, yearning sound which had a pump-like pulse to it. I could not understand the words uttered, and I do not know even if they were words. The sound was neither despairing nor euphoric; it was neither melodic nor was it lacking in musical form; it was, in essence, spiritual.

I retraced my steps a little way and took upon myself the audacity to peer in through a hole in the blinds of a small house, where I saw a man kneeling with tears in his eyes and beads in his hands. I looked only for a moment; then I turned and listened once more. At this point my entire interpretative faculties went into overdrive in an attempt to classify and comprehend this sound.

Was he crying? Was he singing? Was he praying? And the movements I saw him make with his arms? Were they the spontaneous expression of uncontrollable grief? Or were they the orderly gestural accompaniment to worship?

I could not answer any of these questions but could only imagine that the ambiguity and unclassifiable nature of his vocal dance was somehow an important part of why it moved me so much.

In the centre for mentally handicapped adults we went around the circle one by one, each member calling out a sound which the group called back. When it came to Jonathan's turn, something happened that caused me to experience a deep sense of awe. He called out a sound which I had not heard since the time I had stood on that hot dusty street corner in Turkey; and I thought only one thing. If we had taken Jonathan to Turkey and placed him in a room with blinded windows and asked him to call out his sound, passers-by might have asked all kinds of questions. Is he praying? Is he chanting? Is he singing? But they would not for a moment have thought to ask: is he handicapped?

Jonathan's sound was not handicapped. It was full of religiosity, yearning, needing, pleading and worship. It was also full of music. However, because the linguistic content of Jonathan's day-to-day acoustic emissions were not understandable, 'the baby had been thrown out with the bath water' and his entire vocal faculty had been disqualified and rendered insignificant.

In most parts of Europe, singing teachers teach with what they consider to be the indispensable aid of the piano; any vocal sounds made by the student which do not correspond to the black or the white notes are considered unmusical. Western classical music is black and white.

It only takes 15 minutes in Turkey, Egypt, Argentina, India or Bali to discover how limited this view of music is. In those countries whose musical traditions have been unaffected by the black and white philosophy they bend notes in continual defiance of a single pitch.

This is one of the qualities which Jonathan's voice had in common with the man I had heard in Turkey. Jonathan's sounds were not black and white; neither were they meaningless.

I asked Jonathan to wheel himself into the centre of the circle and asked him to sing with me. As he did, I choreographed the perseverative and involuntary movements of his arms which always accompanied his vocalisation into a dance of praying. I had been studying and practically experimenting with various non-western forms of singing for some time and I began to employ some of what I had learned with Jonathan. I began by singing very quietly in such a way as to create the mood and image of a Turkish prayer. I asked Jonathan to sing with me and to develop the movements of his arms into a dance of praying, bending down from the waist in his wheelchair as though kneeling. The group looked on amazed as he composed a voicedance of exquisite authenticity.

It was clear that the wheelchair was restricting him and preventing fluid and liberated physical expression of the imagistic patterns which Jonathan spontaneously yielded. So we helped him out of the chair and into a comfortable kneeling position on the floor. I knelt behind him and held him around the waist with my cheek resting in the small of his back. Together we arose and descended as though in prayer and chanted together in an improvisation of wavering and undulating notes which turned the common room into a sacred space, a temple, a mosque, a synagogue, a church.

I kept repeating Jonathan's sounds back to him with exact replication – except for one thing. Whereas Jonathan sang in Flute, I sang back to him in Saxophone. Eventually, he was able to copy me exactly and his voice tube lengthened and expanded. With this, he lost a certain strain and tension in his voice and its tonal range increased considerably.

After some time, Jonathan became quite excited and enthused by the process, and this was expressed vocally in little spasmodic peeping noises in a falsetto register. I began to mirror these sounds until our musical improvisation gradually transformed into a rhythmical and semi-operatic melody with a xylophone-type quality. In order to ease out the falsetto sounds, I massaged and patted his back, and eventually I was playing his body like a drum. Each time I struck a part of his back, a clear note would emerge.

These notes became stronger, clearer and longer as time went on and it finally became apparent that not only did Jonathan have an awe-inspiring capacity to work in lower pitches, he also had a wonderful upper range akin to a choir boy's.

Over the next eight weeks, Jonathan and his fellows rehearsed with me for a performance based on the story of *Siddhartha* by Hermann Hesse (Bantam Books, 1982). There were no words and no music that was not vocal, apart from the sounds of electric wheelchairs which we incorporated into the composition.

When the stage was set, the lights adjusted, the audience settled and the atmosphere formed, Jonathan wheeled himself out, raised his arms as he did every day, opened his mouth and drooled saliva, as he did every day, and then vocalised continuously as in prayer whilst ten of his peers walked into the performing arena quietly humming. It was so simple, yet it was so moving. And, it was not so much that they were doing anything very different to what they did everyday. It was more that we had managed to shift the perspective of the audience as mine had been shifted in Turkey.

Sometimes, I feel that to educate the ears of the beholder is a more effective approach to Voicework than effecting radical changes in the sounds of the vocalist.

I have taught so many people from such diverse spiritual backgrounds that I have come to realise that I cannot proclaim any connection or insight to the field of the spirit. In my own life I am struggling to be a Christian and this naturally affects me at a deep level. However, it is not something which I incorporate directly into my teaching and I am an advocate of tolerance and mutual respect. For me I believe that Christ is the way, but unlike the good pilgrim, I do not believe that he is the only way. I am also fully aware of the shadow of Christianity – its inexcusable political history and the residue of its intolerance. Such contentions remain my personal struggle.

Photograph 4.1

For myself, I know that in the early days of founding Voice Movement Therapy I worked with many people like Jonathan and sometimes, when faced with those who you know have so little opportunity for change, it is only the sharing of a prayer that gives the courage and determination to go on.

From the Cycles to the Dance

When clients have grasped the rudimentary physical, acoustic and psychological dimensions to the three distinct Developmental Postural Cycles, they are then encouraged to allow the Cycles to blend into a single experience. This happens quite naturally, as clients will inevitably move in and out of personal, archetypal and spiritual realms of experience as they pass through the basic movements. In addition, clients are encouraged to combine the Developmental Postural Cycles with Spherical Space and the Convex and Concave Architecture and use the consequent synthesis as the map, score and tools with which to choreograph and orchestrate a journey which is at once artistically compositional and at the same time authentically psychological in its content (Photographs 4.1). The Developmental Postural Cycles described in this chapter thereby lead naturally into more personalised vocal and movement explorations and set the scene for the next stage of Voice Movement Therapy which seeks to facilitate a combination of natural authentic movement and vocalisation.

In the next chapter I will therefore describe some of the ways in which the movements of the body and the sounds of the voice can be used more spontaneously as a therapeutic tool of self-discovery – for able-bodied and disabled people alike.

CHAPTER 5

Pedestrian Movement, Pedestrian Sound
The Artistic Qualities Inherent in Natural Patterns of Sound and Movement

The Spatial Language of Self

Much of the language which we use to describe our innermost Self is structured around metaphors involving the body in space.

We speak of sticking our neck out, putting our best foot forward, or of not having a leg to stand on. We keep our chin up and our nose clean. We bend over backwards to help someone and we get knocked sideways. We shoulder the blame, swallow our pride, foot the bill and kick the habit. We grasp the opportunity, lick our wounds, side-step the issue and tiptoe around the subject. We wriggle out of our commitments, shake loose from our responsibilities and leap through hoops to find a way out. We shelve ideas, jump into some things and run away from others. We get strung up, come close to the edge, feel boxed in, run around in circles and go up and down like a yoyo. We feel like we are walking on broken glass, skating on thin ice and wading through mud. Things get on top of us, we feel snowed under and pushed into a corner. Life feels like a balancing act, we have too many balls in the air and the carpet gets taken from under our feet. We beat ourselves up over our mistakes and overstretch our resources. Some people waltz through life and others are constantly tripping over themselves.

Images of physicality also play an important role when it comes to describing vocal expression; and our body can feel impacted by what is said to us. We can feel poked, shaken or needled by someone's voice. We can feel tickled by an amusing remark and swiped by an insult. We feel that someone is twisting our arm, poking fun or knocking a hole in our argument. In fact, the sensate impact of language is so great, Freud claimed that words are a substitute for action (Freud 1953–74, Vol.3). When we talk about something which happened in the past, we recreate it and give ourselves a second chance to act; even though this action is only an aspect of spoken recollection.

Language, Art, Sound and Movement

Despite Freud's devoted and exclusive attention to the verbal mode of human expression – which provided the foundations for numerous 'talking cures' – many of our memories, particularly our early memories, are not recalled as a linguistic codified schema. Often there are no words to describe what we recall from the past or what we experience in the present. Instead, many of our deepest and most authentic psychological sensations are an impressionistic matrix which often requires an intuitive, analogical and artistic mode of expression. Van Gogh, Mozart and Caruso painted, composed and sang because, for them, there was no alternative. They could not talk about it. Art emerges from a psychological drive, it is an urgent gesture played out on a continuum from despair to necessity which assumes the only language appropriate to its direction.

But many people feel this urgent drive to discharge the images of their non-verbal psyche – and everybody is surely entitled to create art. Van Gogh was deeply troubled, but compared to some he was lucky. Therapy did not dilute his urgent instinct to paint and life afforded him the brush and the canvas and the time. Had Van Gogh undergone psychotherapy, he might have kept his ear but we might have lost his art.

If the creating of art comes from an urgency only slightly separate from anguish, then what is the role of the arts therapist and what is the relationship between alleviating psychological pain and facilitating the creation of art? Surely, making art is a therapy in itself; for it takes the energetic current of psychological difficulty and creates with it something exquisite, authentic and communicative. When a client of therapy makes art, the personalised inner troubles of the heart and soul become archetypal artifacts which speak to the troubles of the human condition. Art rescues the psyche from isolation even if it does not cure pathology.

The Art of Everyday Life

Sound and movement – or song and dance – are universal art forms which rise up from the core of human experience. So far, a culture has not been discovered that does not sing and does not dance. These acts are part of what it means to be a *Homo sapiens*. But entering a song and dance does not necessarily mean the acquisition of specially learned steps and sounds, which demand a physical virtuosity achievable only by a few. Dance and song are part of the human condition, they are a way of being. When we move, we dance; when we vocalise, we sing. We do these things from the moment we are born.

During the late 1960s and early 1970s a form of modern dance called Pedestrian Movement grew out of the American experimental dance theatre culture. This form of dance took everyday gestures and movements such as walking, sitting, turning, wiping the brow and taking off a hat and amplified them so that they became the vocabulary for original dance performances. This form of dance rarely contained any gymnastic leaps, rolls and tumbles which one might expect from the ballet or the studios of advanced contemporary dance. In many ways, Pedestrian Movement was working against virtuosity. Its social aim was to highlight the dance inherent in the movement of everyday life performed by all people. By amplifying and repeating recognisable gestures and combining them into a choreographic smörgåsbord, the audience were led to reflect upon their own body and their own movements and to consider them as being of artistic and expressive value rather than just functional.

This cultural development within dance was paralleled by a similar interest in everyday noise within experimental music where ringing telephones, tapping typewriters, breaking glass and non-verbal vocal sounds were combined to produce musical performances aimed at pointing to the art in everyday acoustics.

This radical reassessment of the divisions between dance and functional gesture, between music and noise and between a language designed to be upheld by an élite and a language which is truly accessible to anyone offers a useful therapeutic perspective when working with clients with emotional and physical difficulties and restrictions. Such a perspective enables us to see the expressions of the client as an artistic language.

Disabled People Dancing

The term 'Pedestrian Movement', introduced into the dance world during the 1960s to describe the everyday movement patterns of everyday folk, was also referred to at the time as 'found movement'. However, the movement patterns of disabled people were not found at the time. The etymological meaning of 'pedestrian' refers to someone travelling on their feet; and although the pedestrian dance movement challenged the cultural mores of a dance vocabulary, nonetheless all the dancers were able to dance on their feet and disabled people were sadly missing from the dance revolution of the 1960s.

In recent years, however, the notion of Pedestrian Movement has been broadened to include the choreography inherent in bodily movements conditioned by different kinds of physical disabilities. One of the central investigators in this field is Adam Benjamin whose collaboration with Celeste Dandeker led to the formation of the international dance company Candoco.

Celeste Dandeker was a dancer with the London Contemporary Dance Theatre until one night, she fell on stage and broke her neck. The accident left her with a major spinal injury and permanent paralysis. Adam Benjamin was a Tai ch'i teacher who had trained in dance and visual art. He met Celeste and together they began to investigate the notion of a Pedestrian Movement vocabulary accessible to people in wheelchairs.

Photograph 5.1

As Celeste and Adam began dancing together, they found the inherent choreographic art in Celeste's natural bodily movements – which were conditioned by her paralysis. Adam would lie over her lap on the wheelchair as Celeste spun the chair around; Adam would then leap off or roll off the chair and as his body hit the floor, Celeste's arms would rise and carve out a hieroglyphic matrix of gestures in the air.

Inspired by their discoveries, Celeste and Adam began teaching a weekly dance class to a group composed of professional dancers, student dancers and disabled people entirely new to dance.

As a vocabulary of dance developed out of the natural movement patterns of the members, wheelchairs became an asset to the choreographic imagery of the work, opening up completely new kinetic and dramatic opportunities.

This class developed into an internationally acclaimed dance company called Candoco, winning top dance awards and attracting first class choreographers to devise new work for them. As time progressed, new members proved that feet were not a necessary requisite for dance. David Tool, for example, had no feet. In fact he had no legs at all. Yet he could spin, roll, leap, jump and move from one end of the stage to the other on his arms. In fact, he could generate movements which were utterly unachievable by the so-called able-bodied dancers (Photograph 5.1). Celeste's paralysing accident and her collaboration with Adam has led to a performance company which has truly challenged the meaning of 'pedestrian' and 'everyday folk'. These are Adam's reflections.

Adam's Account

For people involved in dance, their medium is the body and their mode of appreciation is aesthetics. Dancers, in many ways, define and redefine who and what is beautiful. The disabled dancer, the dancer who wheels herself on stage in a wheelchair and begins to dance, challenges not only the idea that only the able are able to dance; she also challenges cultural prejudices about human physicality.

The historical, social and cultural treatment of the physically disabled is in many ways the shadow side to the history of western dance. While disabled bodies have been hidden from sight, the well-trained élite of the dance world have been invited to parade before the audience, offering a very one-sided vision of the human body.

My collaboration with Celeste which led to the formation of Candoco and my work now as an educator working with groups integrating disabled and non-disabled people achieves a therapeutic objective through an artistic means.

The arts, including dance, are in crisis. Mainstream dance is certainly losing its way. Art therapy, drama therapy, dance therapy: these seem to be areas in which the arts are once again finding themselves to have purpose and meaning, perhaps because they are returning to their roots. The role of the arts is surely, after all, to allow into our lives and into society those vital yet non-rational parts of what it means to be a human being. In this sense the arts are all about making us whole, allowing us access to our gods and our demons, our capacity to rejoice and celebrate, to experiment and destroy, to express our fears and of course our visions.

If we have separated art therapy from art, drama therapy from drama and dance therapy from dance then there can be little wonder that the mainstream arts are in crisis for it implies that art, drama and dance have been alleviated of their requirement to heal or make whole. I am not a therapist but I think the ultimate achievements of my work have been deeply therapeutic for performers and audience alike.

One of the main psychological issues which disabled dancers have to contend with emanates not from their disability but from the attitude of the audience towards it, which is very often patronising and condescending. The familiar audience response is: 'Aren't they brave. So tragic. It is wonderful to see them up there having a go'. But if you produce dance that is as excellently conceived and executed as any dance performance but which speaks a choreographic language which authentically expresses the nature of the dancers' bodies without apology – such condescension is stopped in its tracks. We're a dance company and the accolades of our achievements have come from the world of performance. We have not had any therapy awards. And this is my whole point; it's what makes our therapeutic objectives possible.

When I make a performance piece and someone who can only move with crutches leaps up and sings, it's dance that is being done and the therapy is inherent.

Disabled People Singing

Through projects which I have led with groups like Candoco, I have found that, in addition to facilitating so-called disabled people in finding their own movement patterns, it is also possible to create moving performance pieces within a group setting which uses voice as a self-accompaniment and which emotionalises the movement. This has the added therapeutic value of enabling people whose bodies are in some ways disabled to draw upon a part of themselves that is highly able, for many people with physical disabilities have voices which are completely agile and fully functional.

The use of voice combined with movement is also a valuable therapeutic tool for use with those who are so-called 'mentally handicapped'. Underneath the obvious and overt language of speech there is a subtle and covert secondary language of voice and movement which communicates the sub-text and undertone to our conscious discourse. This matrix of sounds and gestures emanate from the preverbal phase of infancy when the baby expresses its experience directly through an acoustic gesture, a combination of dance and song. This early form of expression is not codified into a schema capable of being translated from one syntactical logic to another; it is intuitive rather than logical.

Such a form of expression retains its primacy in adulthood amongst those who are generally categorised as 'mentally handicapped' or 'developmentally delayed'. Indeed, there is a variety of congenital impairments to the brain which prohibit the use of speech but which in no way hinder the use of sound and movement. Many of the people I worked with in the early years of developing Voice Movement Therapy were incapable of articulating anything but a few words but nonetheless sang out an orchestra of sound accompanied by a mimetic dance of histrionic gestures.

In adults who simultaneously suffer from a muscular or neuromuscular dysfunction, particularly in hyperkinetic conditions where there is an excess of muscle tension, the expressive movements of the body often appear extremely contorted. In addition, muscle tension has highly detrimental effects on the larynx producing a voice which is strained, tense and which requires great effort to produce.

Very often, the combined vocal and physical pattern of expression in those with inhibited speech and impaired muscle function produces a perseverative song and dance made up of frequently repeated vocal phrases and physical gestures. When working long-term with the same client group, it is natural for professional care workers to become so familiar with such displays that they lose any semblance of meaning. However, what a non-verbal therapeutic strategy such as Voice Movement Therapy can offer is a fresh insight by which the sound and movement patterns can be perceived as an alternative language to verbally articulated thought. Rather than perceiving in the vocal noise and bodily movement of a client only a reminder of the absence of language, it is possible to greet the client with his own language.

When visiting the people of a foreign country whose language we do not speak we would not view the foreign language as an impaired or handicapped use of English. We would stand outside our understanding but nonetheless accept that this strange tongue was coherent and expressive. In order to communicate we would be presented with two choices: to learn the foreign language or to teach English to our foreign friends.

When working with clients for whom the acquisition of verbal language is not an option, the only compassionate choice is to relate to them in their language: that of sound and movement.

This means that the practitioner must first be willing to hear and see the client's expressions as meaningful and expressive. Secondly, the practitioner must be willing to use her own voice and body in the same way as the client, to share in the non-formal language of voice and movement.

About ten years ago I took a job as director of Libra Theatre Company. The company was composed of a group of people, each of whom had a major disability or condition which seriously compromised their health. In the group were people with Multiple Sclerosis, people paralysed due to major accidents, people who could not see, people who could not hear, people who could not speak and many people who could not walk. Yet they could all give voice. In fact, when I first entered the room to meet the group the noise level was incredible.

On the first day, we went around the circle and listened to each person call out, as though singing out from a mountain top. Then at the end, we all joined together to chant a single note in a circle. Arms gyrated, legs kicked, saliva drooled and eyes gleamed as this group of people with nothing in common joined with one another in an acoustic communion which moved me to tears. Over the next six months we met every Saturday to build a performance. There were no words; just movements and voices.

Working with Libra taught me that voice can be a great equaliser and that when working with disabled bodies, the voice is a way of bringing the able Self to the surface. When working with severely disabled people or people with serious conditions such as Multiple Sclerosis, the voices often reveal a great vibrancy. One of the most rewarding things about working through voice is that people who are physically immobilised can travel through sound. Expanding the range of the voice and touring its contours provides an opportunity to take a journey through the terrain of the heart – without leaving the spot (Photograph 5.2).

Practical Method: Walk, Wheel, Sing and Dance

Working with a group of people, some of whom are in wheelchairs and some of whom can walk, the practitioner firstly asks the group of people to walk or wheel from one end of the studio to the other. Then, secondly, the practitioner asks them to walk or wheel from one end to the other one at a time so that the group can observe each other.

Contained in this simple exercise is a fascinating wealth of information that testifies to the diversity of human personality. For no two people walk or wheel as much as three feet in the same way. Some people walk or wheel quickly and others slowly. Some walk or wheel as though motivated to arrive whilst others appear to be getting away from what is behind them. Some people look at the floor, some at the sky and others straight ahead. Some people seem to be led by the right foot or right wheel, others by the left. Some people tense their arms, others grip their hands tightly shut; some

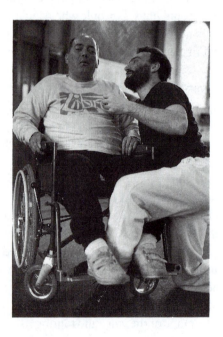

Photograph 5.2

people hold their abdominal wall taut, others swank or roll along with a relaxed belly. Some people breathe in rhythm with their walking or wheeling, others maintain a cycle of breath which remains barely influenced by the kinetics of walking or wheeling. Some seem to be gravitationally rooted to the floor or to the chair whilst others seem to float on thin air.

After the group has watched each person walk and wheel, the practitioner helps the group identify basic differences in walking and wheeling style between members of the group and invites the group members to reflect upon their own manner of walking or wheeling and upon the walking and wheeling style of others in the group. In the aftermath of this discussion, the practitioner invites the group to once again walk and wheel around the studio all together. This time, the participants notice the various elements of their walking or wheeling, experiencing the factors which go to make up the composition of their unique style of travel.

As with all aspects of physical movement, the elements of any style of walking and wheeling reflect psychological factors. Travelling with the sensation of floating on thin air creates a different sense of Self to a mode of travelling which is rooted to the ground. Travelling with a respiratory pattern synonymous with the rhythm of the steps or the rotation of the wheels feels very different to travelling with a pattern of breathing which remains in its own groove. The sense of attention which one has when travelling whilst looking at the ground is different to that which one has when looking upwards or forwards. Although these things are incredibly simple, they are central to the way that psychological condition is influenced by physical movement and the way physical movement is shaped by psychological state.

To enable each person to investigate which aspects of their Self are expressed through their way of walking or wheeling, the practitioner asks the clients to amplify the elements of their travelling style, taking time to exaggerate their steps, creating a character or a caricature. The practitioner then gives the group a chance to observe each participant present their exaggerated or amplified travelling character, as one by one each member moves around the studio before their audience.

Afterwards, the participants are asked to consider whether their exaggerated style of travelling symbolises the way they 'move through life' and if so how. As the group begin to share with one another their experience of amplifying the simple notion of travelling, each participant can sense the potential of a simple movement exercise like this to open up insights into the nature of their Self.

Now, the practitioner asks the group to return to moving around the studio exploring their amplified walking or wheeling pattern, whilst vocalising, firstly on a long continuous sound and then using a compositional babble. The participants are then invited to explore the range of their voice, finding a character of voice which accompanies and reflects the characteristics of their style of travel.

In searching for a distinct vocal character, clients are encouraged to use the various component ingredients of their voice and in particular to locate their character in one of the three voice timbres of Flute, Clarinet and Saxophone. As a result, each member of the group develops a quality of vocalisation which brings further amplification to their creative expression of a characterised aspect of themselves. These vocal characters are then presented one by one to the witnessing group and an opportunity to share experiences is offered.

A particular travelling style and voice may have originated from a psychological state. On the other hand, a psychological state may be engendered and sustained by our physical and vocal expressions which have emerged from necessity. Regardless of whether chicken or egg came first, the fact remains that transforming the way we move and vocalise within the boundaries of our limitations has the potential to transform our sense of Self.

So returning to practical work, the group is asked to take their caricatured travelling style and quality of voice once more and move through the studio all together. As they do this, they are asked to begin to allow the elements of their walking and wheeling and the components of their voice to turn into their opposites. A fast pace becomes a slow stroll; a quick and aggressive turn of the wheel become a nonchalant glide; a downward glance becomes an upward stare; a sense of gravity becomes a sense of flight; a sense of moving away from something becomes a sense of moving towards something; a sense of right foot or wheel forward becomes a sense of being led by the left side; a forward stoop becomes a backward arch; gripped hands become flat. Meanwhile, a high-pitched voice lowers, a voice with lots of free air becomes solidified; a voice in modal register changes to falsetto register; a loud voice becomes quiet and a Flute Timbre becomes a Saxophone Timbre.

Once again, the group takes a rest as each person presents their new style of travel and new quality of voice to their audience. Afterwards, the group is given an opportunity to share with each other their experience of exploring an unfamiliar way of vocalising and moving through the studio as a metaphor for adopting an unfamiliar way of moving through life and giving voice to their Self in the world. This moving and vocalising exercise is extremely simple and can be conducted with any clientele capable of walking or wheeling and voicing.

The final stage of this investigation involves inviting clients to make the transition from a sense of travelling to a sense of dance.

Most forms of traditional dance are an adaptation and elaboration of the simple act of walking: the waltz, the fox-trot, the tango, the quickstep, Flamenco and the twist all utilise particular ways of walking and travelling. Moreover, each dance form suggests a different emotional atmosphere which is enhanced by the vocal music which accompanies the movement. However, the sentiments, the ambience and the passion of these dance forms are not and should not only be accessible to those who can move on their feet. The tango, for example, originates in the downtrodden troubles of the disenfranchised people of Argentina. We do not need feet to relate to this.

To begin, the practitioner asks the group to return to one end of the studio and travel on foot or in chair from one end to the other whilst listening to some Flamenco deep song. Then the group walks again whilst listening to a fox-trot. The exercise is then repeated, each time accompanied by a different kind of dance music.

The practitioner then brings the group into a circle and asks each member to create a single tone which combines with the tones of each member of the group in harmony. This provides a supportive sonorous envelope of sound. Then, in pairs, two clients enter the circle walking and wheeling around one another allowing the style of travel to turn into a dance, influenced by the sentiments of one of the dance forms explored to music earlier. The dancers then begin to vocalise using a compositional babble of vowels and consonants, creating an improvisation which yields a vocal improvisation synonymous in mood and tempo to the movements of the dance. This exploration tends to create a celebrational mood and it is always fascinating how different pairs produce song and dance routines with fundamentally different temperaments. When a person in a chair dances with a person on foot, the most moving and stunning sculptural and acoustic images are often made, as the chair becomes an added artistic feature. Moreover, there are speeds, turns, twists and glides possible on wheels which are not possible on feet and this turns the wheelchair into a physical advantage.

To close the process, each pair is invited to share their experience of presenting their song and dance, including an exploration of how and why they produced particular temperaments, tempos and ambience and any issues which arose through the process.

Practical Method: Repetition and Composition

I have worked with clients who continually bite their nails, with those who repeatedly chew their lip or brush their hair from their face or scratch their arm or fiddle with their wedding ring or tap their foot or rub their hands. A therapeutic perspective very often pathologises such behaviour as compulsive. Yet in the field of choreographic composition, this is how dance is made.

In choreography, a dancer takes a simple movement, often very tiny to begin with, and then begins to amplify it to involve the whole body. This movement is then repeated and combined with other repeated movements and it is in the repetition that it becomes compositional.

In Voice Movement Therapy, the so-called compulsive gestures of the client are amplified to make the vocabulary for a dance. And the same approach is applied to the voice. For, just as we have gestures which we tend to repeat, so each of us has an acoustic vocabulary of gasps and sighs, words and phrases which make up our everyday vocal dance. Again, by encouraging these to be amplified and combined, a vocal score is created.

When clients are enabled to take their everyday gestures and sounds and understand them as a vocabulary with which to create a choreography and a score, their artistic aspirations can be rescued from beneath what may otherwise seem to be the futile and meaningless histrionics of everyday life.

From the Dance to the Deeps

For both able-bodied and disabled people, voice and movement provide an opportunity to journey through the Self. By highlighting the grace and artistic integrity inherent in everyday gestures and task-orientated ways of travelling, clients can come to appreciate their creative potential as their predicament becomes celebrated rather than pathologised. In this process, the use of specific musical and choreographic forms, such as those referred to above, provides a particular kind of container for self-exploration. However, once someone begins to combine movements and sounds freely and spontaneously, then it is as though the client has begun a journey which can bring the light and dark of the psyche to the surface in a highly vivid manner. Gestures and sounds can imply self-mutilation or can express instinctive aggression. A particular turn of the head combined with a certain quality of voice can unleash fathomless sorrow. Furthermore, a certain combination of sound and movement may remind the client of a specific trauma and possibly even re-traumatise them. On the other hand, working deeply with sound and movement can also enable positive emotions and sensations to replace negative ones through the process of replacing self-effacing or self-negating sounds and movements with those that are self-confident and self-affirming.

Regardless of the direction, working through sound and movement soon becomes a journey of equal depth, meaning and magnitude to the journey taken through words by the static client of psychoanalysis. And this journey needs to be guided with care and sensitivity, with accuracy and compassion. It is therefore the notion of a journey through sound and movement that forms the next stage in the Voice Movement Therapy methodology and to which I will now turn my attention in the next chapter.

CHAPTER 6

The Voice Movement Journey
Touring the Contours of the Psyche through Authentic Sound and Movement

The Pilgrim, the Artist and the Seeker of Therapy

The pilgrim journeys towards spiritual enlightenment. He searches for god, for the wisdom of the Buddha, for a peace of mind and a stillness of soul. To make such a search the pilgrim must be ready to embark upon a journey of frustration, disappointment, fear and excitement during which all things most common and most familiar will be challenged and set aside. The pilgrim walks barefoot with no protection from the ground; and the pain of the soil beneath the feet ensures that the pilgrim will not lose touch with the earth in his search for the skies. The pilgrim's journey is made up mainly of routine, regularity and commitment: early to bed and early to rise, regular meals of modest proportion, prayer or meditation and lots and lots of walking and searching.

The artist shares many aspects of life with the pilgrim. The artist searches to find the purest and most authentic expression of our quintessential being, our soul. To walk the way of the artist is to follow the pilgrim beyond the walls of the populace, to give up the profane dictates of social discourse and the status quo and devote one's life to a journey, a search. But, like the pilgrim, the artist's life is one of routine and commitment: the dancer must train his body, the actor must repeat his lines, the musician must practise his scales. And, like the journey of the pilgrim, the artist's journey is also filled with loneliness, fear and disappointment. Yet, like the pilgrim, the artist can touch moments of divine inspiration when the nature of the world may, for a few moments, seem to be made apparent with utmost clarity.

The person in search of therapy must be prepared to join the pilgrim and the artist. For therapy is a journey through the ever-changing terrain of the psyche where the landscape comprises swamp and mountain, ditch and desert, forest and jungle. Many people who come into therapy have not realised that, if they continue with their desire, they will be departing from all that is familiar and taking a safari. To survive this safari, the basics are essential: commitment, routine and a willingness to greet all emotions with equal prudence.

Commitment is a prerequisite for a therapeutic journey; for just as God will not appear for the pilgrim at first, second or third request, so the grail which the client seeks may elude him for days, weeks, months. Yet, often, on a therapeutic journey, though the goal of one's search seems to be ungraspable, other more unexpected discoveries do occur; some of them unpleasant, some of them threatening and others enlightening. The therapist must enable the client to greet all the feelings which arise equally: boredom, fear, anxiety, rage, emptiness and excitement. These do not relate according to a hierarchy; they occupy equal places in the spherical fabric of human experience.

For therapy to be effective, the therapist must enable the client to learn from what is there and help the client avoid being blinded by the wish that something else had been discovered instead. This can only be done if therapy is routine and followed with a labour-like dedication. Between here and Kilimanjaro or Jericho or Nirvana is a long road and there are only so many miles you can travel in a day. But if you never set foot on the road and do not continue travelling through all weathers, Kilimanjaro or Jericho or Nirvana remain references in a book, dots on a postcard and places which, in the final hours, we regret never having visited.

In psychoanalysis and most forms of psychotherapy, the vehicle of the client's journey is the couch. The client reclines and closes his eyes and begins talking. He talks of his feelings and moods, of his dreams and desires, of his relatives, family and friends, of his preoccupations and worries. When the client becomes involved in this tour, he forgets the walls of the consulting room and the stasis of the couch and seems to travel through space and time, visiting and revisiting new and ancient territory. The speech of the client is an improvisation, like a monologue of an actor without a script who simply follows an artistic intuition.

Though the therapist may intervene, momentarily turning a monologue into a dialogue, much of what the client discovers is uncovered through his own listening. By listening to the Self as it unfolds, the client realises the surreptitious map which guides the unravelling of the Self. At these moments, the client lingers longer at junctions and crossroads contemplating whether to make a different choice which will lead down a different path.

In Voice Movement Therapy, as in psychotherapy, the client takes a journey which is directed by the improvising intuition of the client himself. However, in Voice Movement Therapy, the vehicle is not the couch and the medium is not words. Rather, the vehicle is the open plane of the studio and the medium is voice and movement. This is called a Voice Movement Journey.

There are two kinds of Voice Movement Journey: the Guided Voice Movement Journey and the Unguided Voice Movement Journey. In the Guided Voice Movement Journey the practitioner is instrumental in steering the process, influencing sounds and moves in the manner of a choreographer, conductor, director, masseur and voice coach. In the Unguided Voice Movement Journey, the practitioner is primarily a witness as the client improvises in a self-directed manner.

Practical Method: The Guided Voice Movement Journey

In a Guided Voice Movement Journey, which is ideally suited to a one-to-one session, the practitioner combines the elements of a number of roles including psychotherapist, masseur, singing teacher, voice coach, theatre director and choreographer.

For example, the therapist asks the client to sing, without effort or tension, without demonstration or histrionics. She sings as herself. The patient utters first this note, then that, ascending and descending a scale in which the practitioner can hear or imagines she can hear distinct qualities. For the practitioner, from the perspective of a subjective counter-transference, the sound may appear genial and tender with a wispy emission of free air; the higher the pitch the more gentle, soft and unassertive it becomes. It has a girlish frivolity and fragile delicacy to it. The practitioner can see that the client is swaying slightly from side to side and has an ingenuous expression on her face that seems to enhance the innocence of the sound. The practitioner asks the patient to exaggerate the swaying as though she were on a swing and to increase the child-like quality of the voice, as though she were only seven years old. The client begins to enter into the embodiment of this image and the practitioner leads the client's pitch up the scale into a higher octave to assist in excavating and refining a sonic and authentic neonatal and infantile image. As the notes begin to get higher, and more difficult to sing, the client contorts the face and clenches her fists which serves to bring to the quality of the sound a degree of ruckus and commotion, as though the baby were having a tantrum. The practitioner asks the client to sing as though the baby were spoilt, irritable, incensed and protesting, and as a result the indignant spectacle becomes more animated and multiphonic. The client opens and closes her fists, stamps on the ground and the practitioner now massages and manoeuvres the neck and back in order to ward off unnecessary tension in the relevant muscle groups. The client continues to vocalise during this massage; her voice increases considerably in volume and height on the pitch scale and whistles through the studio like a siren.

In order to facilitate the sensible experience and personification of the instinctive, natal and primal quality which is emerging, the practitioner asks the client to move into a Feline-canine position and to dance the back and shoulders in an undulating ripple of waves to ensure freedom of corporeal action. The practitioner rhythmically massages the abdominal wall and requests that the client imagine that she howls as though from the abdomen and that the sound resonates inside her belly which is lined with white gold. The sound now assumes a canine quality like that of a howling wolf. The practitioner asks the client to imagine that her hackles are up and that she howls a warning and protecting shield of sound around her cubs, which lie curled beneath her belly. The pitch descends and the sound becomes guttural and marauding and echoes as though in a cave. In the deeper pitches the sound is wolf-like; in the higher pitches it is feline; in the middle there is an ambiguous animalistic quality, half wolf, half cat, like a beast from a beguiling world of creatures concocted from an amalgam of animal instincts.

The practitioner, having paid passive attention to the client's tendency to open and close the fists during this vocal dance, now asks the client to develop this movement as though she were a creature extending and retracting her claws in preparation for a fight. At the same time she is asked to decrease the volume of the sound and to sing with an alluring, tantalising and ravenous tone, part lion, part Siamese kitten, part wolf. As the client sings, the practitioner continues to suggest tonal images: feline, predatory, devouring, spiteful, provocative, protective. The creature has offspring and is prowling around her young. She spits, with venom, with foreboding and intimidation. Her voice is made of acid, it is caustic, ungracious and scathing.

The practitioner now influences the melodic direction of the sounds by singing different notes. As the vocal dance assumes a more formal structure, the sounds become humanised without losing their arresting and compelling intensity. The client stands and the therapist suggests the image of a gigantic Parisian chain-smoking animal lover with six children who wears a cape and bellows and bawls. The client's voice becomes darkly enfolding which the practitioner amplifies by suggesting a collage of images: mouth full of caviar, a voice like molasses or like tar, an attitude of belligerent certainty. The voice is that of a prolific and world-famous Parisian lion-tamer. A new character emerges and the studio now thunders with the voice of 'Madam Felineou'. The client now struts around the studio singing improvised arias on the words 'I am Madam Felineou', like a prima donna. She mimes smoking with a cigarette holder. Her whole face has altered radically from the attitude it expressed at the beginning of the session and any visible or vocal signs of innocence and vulnerability have long since receded. The voice and physicality of the client is dominant, proud and unnerving.

The practitioner watches the movements of the arm which mime the backwards and forwards motion of putting cigarette to mouth and asks the client to magnify and inflate it. It becomes now the whip that spurs the horses and the client is now driving a chariot away from the circus into the forest. The voice now takes on a hot-blooded, ambitious and barbarous tone. The practitioner encourages this transformation by suggesting tonal images: Boadicea, the wild woman of the forest, revengeful war cry, leading the warriors into battle, rounding up a tribal mass of agitated protesters. The client's voice and body is now involved in an opera of blood-curdling melody as though the studio were full with an army of female rebels.

The client is becoming tired, and the practitioner slows down the pace through gentle instruction. The dead lie scattered and the wild woman now feels sorrow for the victims. The voice returns to a higher pitch and whimpers. The practitioner suggests tonal images: pangs of regret, mourning and melancholy; a prayer for the dying and a contemplative chant on the futility of war. The client now stands swaying, as she was at the beginning of the session and the practitioner asks her to blend in different aspects of the acoustic journey into a single tone. The irritable child, the vulnerable kitten, the howling wolf, the wild woman of the forest, Madam Felineou and the unbridled warrior become less separate and distinct voices and more aspects audible in a single tone. The voice sounds and feels to practitioner and client that it belongs to her. But it is multi-faceted, embracing and containing a spectrum of images any one or combination of which could emerge as the dominant factor at any time.

The process of transformation from this wolf image to the image of Madam Felineou is a slow one, in which every stage of the transformation from the howling wolf to the meowing cat-woman is fleshed out, filled in, satiated and made specific through precise alterations in acoustic quality and kinetic gesture. From wolf to wolf-dog and then to wolf-cat; from wolf-cat to cat and from cat to cat-woman; and finally from cat-woman to the cat-like woman, Madam Felineou. This has nothing to do with the generalised mimicry of putting on different voices, such as that heard in pastiche cabaret, and when the vocalist succumbs to the superficial option of mimicry, not only the attuned practitioner and the client but anyone else who may be present in a group session can hear it.

The professional practitioner must help to amplify, embellish, fertilise, enrich and refine the timbral qualities which are present in the voice but must not generalise and abstract all detail; he must remain attentive to specifics, which requires acute listening. Furthermore, the practitioner must not be influenced by his own modalities or imagistic preoccupations. He must not trespass eagerly forward according to his own tastes. He must not adorn and decorate through suggestions which emanate from the prejudice of his own ears. The images supplied by the practitioner must originate in the acoustic information supplied by the client and must be amplified to embody images of a genuine significance, culturally and personally, and not to reflect the widespread social stereotypes to which modern men and women have become prey. This requires of the practitioner an intimate and well-tested exploration of his or her own subjective reactions, that is his or her counter-transference.

The advantage of a Guided Voice Movement Journey is that an able practitioner can intervene and enable the client to avoid employing unhealthy methods of voice production and avoid repeating patterns of vocalisation which compound restriction and inhibition. The disadvantage of the Guided Voice Movement Journey is that the client is steered directively and is not completely free to experience the contours of the psyche uninfluenced by the witness. This is why it is important to balance such journeys with Unguided Voice Movement Journeys.

Practical Method: The Unguided Voice Movement Journey

The Unguided Voice Movement Journey is a process which can be taken by a single client or by a group of clients witnessed by the practitioner.

The client begins by choosing a position – standing, sitting or lying – which reflects their present state of mind, mood, preoccupation or feeling. They then begin breathing in and out through the mouth imagining that the breath fills the body with air. Then, they begin toning a single note, allowing the pitch to rise and descend, the loudness to increase and decrease and allowing the other timbral ingredients of the voice to come and go. As they sound, they take a simple movement which in some way expresses their impulse, instinct and improvising intuition at that moment. It may be an everyday familiar gesture; it may be a sudden roll or turn or jump; it may be a change of position from standing to sitting, from lying to standing or from sitting to lying; or it may be a travelling motion through space.

The client then allows the original sound and the original movement to combine and elaborate, forming a wordless song and dance routine or voicedance. As clients vocalise and dance, a scenario may emerge: they may feel as though they are a child back in the family environment expressing particular attitudes such as irritability, rage or disappointment. They may feel as though they are becoming a different character, as though acting in a drama and this character may seem to be an amplification of a specific sub-personality. They may feel that they are reliving a specific event such as a traumatic experience or a peak moment of joy and discovery. Or they may feel that they are plotting out the contours of their emotional landscape through voice and movement, like an abstract painter would do through shape and colour upon the canvass.

The Voice Movement Journey is a very individual experience, though each journey taken by all clients has in common the use of improvised movement and improvised sound as the medium of expression and exploration. The following are some accounts by people who have taken an Unguided Voice Movement Journey, showing the diversity of experience.

To begin, let us return to Martin.

Client's Account: Martin

In the Corner Stands the Boxer

Because I had discovered a lot of anger during the Convex and Concave work, I decided that I would try to revisit these angry feelings in the Unguided Voice Movement Journey. I started moving through Convex and Concave, walking forward and back, vocalising on a single note. After a while, I noticed again the way that I would have feelings of panic and fear when the front of my body was concave and feelings of anger and rage when the front of my body was convex. When in concave, my voice sounded shaky and stuck, reminding me again of my normal speaking tone. But when in convex, my voice became loud, like a calling sound. As I went back and forth from convex and concave, I noticed how my head was pulled back and my chest was pushed out in convex; and this was a familiar position for me from when I took boxing lessons at a gym some years ago. At the same time, my loud, open, calling voice reminded me of a sailor or a fisherman yelling to haul up the sails and I thought of the song: 'What Shall We Do With The Drunken Sailor?'

I now started exaggerating the boxing movements and playing with my voice using the tune of 'What Shall We Do With The Drunken Sailor?' I felt incredibly powerful, masculine and strong, like a bull. I kept vocalising and dancing, light on my feet but heavy in my arms. I started to sing the words to the song, and I did not stutter at all.

Then I remembered the work with Spherical Space and my feelings of being hemmed in and in a flash the sense of what I was doing changed. Now I felt like I was trying to box my way out of a small room. Then I started to have panicked feelings and began to imagine that the room was on fire, filling with smoke; and I couldn't breathe. Even though my chest was convex, my voice began to constrict and I started coughing and gagging.

Now I started feeling angry at myself. I felt weak. But I gave in to it. I went back to concave, retuned to the centre of the sphere and like a big baby, I started sobbing.

Then an incredible thing happened. I got so angry at myself for sobbing, yet at the same time I felt so upset at losing my 'boxer voice' that I stood up and started singing at the top of my voice in a tone that was a mixture of anger and sorrow. It was a quality of voice I had heard in some jazz singers before, particularly in songs about the slave movement when the voice makes you feel the outrage and the grief at the same time. I felt as though two opposite feelings had blended and a new voice had emerged.

When we talked about our experiences in the group, I realised a number of important things. When I was young, all my brothers were much more intelligent than I was. I was the sort of dunce of the family. I tried to compensate for this by being good at sport and by being physically strong – as they were all quite lean and tender and academic. But I was no better at physical things than I was at mental things. Plus, I had my stutter which made me feel even more of an outcast. I was suffocated by my family's overbearing academic demands and over-emphasis on achievement. I tried to box my way out but just felt too weak and ended up crying. I must have cried an ocean of tears as a child.

This is why I don't push my kids to be what they are not.

Client's Account: Philip

Sobbing for the World

When I began the Unguided Voice Movement Journey I had no idea what I was going to do. I just knew that I had been feeling sad all day – for no apparent reason.

I began walking very slowly, toning a single note, rubbing my hands together as though I was cold. For a fleeting moment I had an image of myself as a Russian peasant on the freezing plains of the Eastern Bloc, like in those epic films about the Russian revolution. I began singing in Saxophone using lots of strange throaty sounds like 'ach' and 'schsh'. As I sang, the sadness which I had been feeling all day became more intense and for some reason I started thinking about my mother who died about ten years ago. I stared singing in a sort of Russian accent: 'mumma sha, mumma sha'. Impulsively I knelt down and started opening and closing my arms, periodically looking up at the sky. I felt like I was at a funeral, only by now I had stopped thinking about my mother and was just feeling grief-stricken in a general sense. I started to feel like I was singing and sobbing for the sorrow of the world and tears began to run down my face. I don't think I had heard my voice like this before – rich, deep, dark and full of a pathos that was strangely unfamiliar to me.

Yet, although I felt so much grief it also felt incredibly soothing. I am a journalist and I am always reporting on tragedies of one kind or another. After a while you start to write up grief-ridden stories with no feeling. I wondered, after the Voice Movement Journey, where I put the feelings that I must surely have in response to the stories I encounter through my work. During the Voice Movement Journey, it felt like I had an opportunity to vocalise and sing out the grief that I cannot show in my professional life.

I had come into therapy to get in touch with my feelings, having grown tired of my intellectual, passionless, over-educated front that everybody seemed to see. I knew that there was an 'emotional me' somewhere. I just didn't realise how deeply I could feel sorrow and how fully I could express it through my voice. It will be difficult for me to disguise my sorrow in future.

Client's Account: Vicky

Ungluing the Voice

As a child I was repeatedly abused by my father who made me engage in oral sex. The memories are very vivid, particularly the feeling of numb helplessness in my body as my father knelt on my arms to keep me down.

I came to work on myself through voice and movement because, although psychotherapy had enabled me to deal with and overcome many of the issues and heal some of the damage, some problems remained. The main problem was a feeling of tightness in my throat and an incredibly inhibited voice. Whenever I came to project my voice or speak up about something important, I would feel a stickiness in my throat, as though my voice was covered with something that made it dull and unable to flow fluidly.

At the beginning of the Voice Movement Journey my first impulse was to get onto the floor, lying on my side in a kind of fetal position. Then, when I began making my initial single tone I noticed that I put one hand around my throat and started rubbing it. So, I decided to make this my starting movement. The combination of the sound and the throat-rubbing movement made me feel a mixture of rage, frustration and an incredible sense of unfairness. I heard everyone around me increase the loudness of their sounds and the voices seemed to have such a mixture of qualities. Mine just seemed monotone, quiet and stuck. I got so angry at this that I started rolling over, first to one side and then to the other, like a baby trying to get out of its crib. I then extended the gesture of rubbing my throat, bringing my arm out in front of me and swinging it back in towards the throat as if pulling glue out of my voice box. I then started to make gluing sounds, like the sounds which children make when they pretend to be speaking underwater. I was crying by this time but also quite manic, as though if I kept pulling and pulling, eventually all the glue would go and my voice would emerge fresh and unstuck.

As I began to hear my 'glue voice' I had a startling recognition. The voice was like the speaking voice which emerged whenever I tried to project my voice or speak out. I wanted to test this, so I stood up and began walking about the studio vocalising a gobbledygook made-up language in the voice that was my familiar 'stuck speaking voice'. My neck felt tight and I began exaggerating this tightness, making ostrich-like movements with my head. As I reached the back of the studio, I slid down the wall and returned to my fetal position. I felt very depressed and quite tired. All I could manage was tiny movements of my jaw, as though I was chewing cud. However, as I indulged these minimal movements, I noticed the sound of my voice change from a gluey quality to a more clear shiny quality as the pitch went up. I stared to feel a 'melting sensation' in my throat and a feeling of release.

I felt the depressive sensation lift and a moment of hope and joy filled me with a smile; and I began singing a tune which just popped into my head. I think it must have been the tune to a nursery rhyme.

I felt that my journey had ended and I could feel the atmosphere in the room settle as most people seemed to be coming to the end of their journeys.

When we came together to talk a little about our experiences, I felt that the sensation of melting which had come from the gentle chewing movements and the soft nursery rhyme singing were an important key for me. The violent pulling movements and gluey sounds which came from my urgent desire to pull away the stuck sensation seemed to be as aggressive towards myself as my father had been in his abuse. As I began talking about this I found myself crying at the realisation that there really was no one who had been kind to me as a child and I was really not very kind to myself as an adult. Perhaps kind sounds and movements would enable my glue to melt without the need to rip it off.

Diversity of Journeys

These accounts show the diversity of journeys which clients can take when they are witnessed but unguided. It is very important, however, that the practitioner watches and listens carefully to each member of the group to ensure that no one is repeating modes of vocal expression which are threatening to the physiological health and longevity of the vocal instrument. It is also important that the practitioner is aware when a client has touched upon something or unearthed something in an Unguided Voice Movement Journey which may need more directive work if the material is to be appropriated, understood and explored. Often clients will describe a discovery which they made during an Unguided Journey which begs for further work so obviously that to leave it untouched would make the journey, in retrospect, more damaging than health-enhancing.

The case of Vicky was an example of a situation which I felt needed such personal directive attention.

Case Study: Vicky

A Journey Through Song and Sperm

After the Voice Movement Journey session in which Vicky explored a way to unglue her voice and rescue it from the psychosomatic results of oral sexual abuse, I asked participants to write their experience of their journey in the form of a simple rhyming song. When Vicky came to present her piece, she sang: 'Sperm and cream it makes me scream cos daddy made me suck at his big Jimmy Dean' to the child-like nursery rhyme melody she had spontaneously invented during her Unguided Voice Movement Journey.

After we had heard the songs of each participant I worked with Vicky in an individual Voice Movement Therapy session. Before we began, Vicky explained that during the Unguided Voice Movement Journey she had explored expelling the sperm, wiping it away and refusing to take it in. Later, she had found herself making small, gentle masticatory movements and sounds which she described as 'melting sounds'. It was during this time that she found herself singing a child-like melody and remembering how she used to sing to herself as a means of comfort after her father had left the room following an abusive episode. However, she had also, ironically, experienced a loss of vocal expression as an adult. Indeed, when she explained why she had come to work on herself through Voice Movement Therapy she described the sensation of something being 'glued to her voice' preventing it from 'coming out'. As she described this she began to cry and sob as her body undulated and quivered in spasm. I thus began to work with her, facilitating her development of the masticatory jaw movements combined with her singing her song. This gave me the impression of someone trying to sing whilst chewing.

I directed her body back and forth from a concave implosion to a convex protrusion at the front and this instigated her to spit out saliva, as though expelling sperm. As we worked, her body became extremely hot and she sweated profusely. Then, at a point of quite vigorous expulsive movement, her voice changed from Flute Timbre to Clarinet Timbre as the voice tube expanded. Simultaneously, her voice changed register from falsetto to modal and it became very disrupted, like a rough, gritty growl. I asked her to amplify this disrupted sound and allow the song to develop, in response to which she sang the words: 'It's not sweet, even though it's white', over and over again. In time, the song developed into a whole verse which attacked the father with contempt and rage. The song finished with lines which accused him of 'spoiling her ice cream' with the sperm from 'his big Jimmy Dean'.

I asked her now to sing the song as though her voice was melting ice cream; and she sung the song in a deep, rich Saxophone Timbre voice. She could have been singing the blues.

For this client the process of working simultaneously through catharsis, bodily movement and sung words was extremely beneficial. For, she had reached a point in her psychoanalytic treatment where the repetitious verbal analysis of the problem had most definitely served the purpose of enabling her to withdraw negative projections and displaced anger towards men, originating from her father's abuse. Yet, it had not solved the problem of her voice, which still felt like something was glued to it. By combining Guided and Unguided Voice Movement Journeys with psychophysical work she was able to alleviate the stuck feeling in the throat and reclaim her full voice, liberating it from the muscular manifestation of sexual abuse.

Before, During and After

Like all safaris, there are inevitable and universal feelings which arise in the client before, during and after a Voice Movement Journey.

Before a journey, two of the common feelings are trepidation and fear of nothingness. The client does not know where to start, what sound to make and what part of the body to move. She looks around her and witnesses others in the group making headway and this makes her feel worse. In some cases, this can lead to extreme self-consciousness which has a paralysing effect on voice and body. Of course, from the perspective of the witnessing practitioner, the client has already begun. Her self-consciousness and feelings of paralysis manifest in facial expressions, gestures and postures which constitute the beginning of her journey. While the client is wondering when her feelings will pass so she can begin her journey, her journey has in fact commenced. Her breathing pattern, too, will be reflective of her state of mind and mood and if the client just amplifies the breathing a little, sounds will emerge that will start the acoustic dimension of the Voice Movement Journey.

Another state of mind which often leads clients to feel blocked and unable to begin their journey is boredom, particularly amongst clients in long-term therapeutic work for whom the novelty of the Voice Movement Journey has long since receded. Again, however, boredom is a perfectly viable emotional starting point for a journey. In fact, boredom is one of the most virile emotions. Unlike the obvious emotions like anger and grief which everyone in therapy loves to speak about and access and express, boredom lingers like a shadow. Boredom is an emotion we try to escape, as though it is irrelevant or does not really belong in the list of human passions. Yet boredom is a volcano. Boredom ignites people, agitates people, frustrates people, leads people to get anxious, uncomfortable, angry, tired, excited and above all, boredom forces change – for everyone seeks to relieve themselves of boredom.

Boredom also poses a challenge to a practitioner. There is a particular pressure on practitioners who lead groups to keep their group engaged which can easily dupe the leader into thinking that he must entertain. Some inexperienced group leaders panic when they think members of their group are bored and seek to relieve the boredom and recapture the clients' interest. This is part of boredom's trickery. Boredom makes itself known through its powers of repulsion. Boredom knows that it is ugly and that as soon as it shows its face we will turn away lest we be turned to stone. Consequently, boredom is rarely faced, rarely challenged and rarely neutralised. Yet, when we do have the courage to greet boredom, face it and feel it, it is denied its powers of repulsion and retreats, exposing the underlying reservoir of passions. The group leader must not seek to calm his own sense of inadequacy by relieving the group's boredom.

Another emotion which arises during the course of a Voice Movement Journey for many clients is fear. Once a client is enabled to lengthen and dilate the vocal tract and achieve maximum dexterity of the vocal instrument, there seems to be no end to the emotions, images and psychic contents which come flooding out of the mouth in all acoustic shapes and sizes. Most clients will never have heard themselves like this before. They feel a power, a resilience and an enormity and this can be quite terrifying. One of the reasons for the terror often lies in the client's fear of being destructive. Unfortunately, many people have only encountered power in the form of tyranny. Many of us have tasted another person's power when they have been destructive towards us and, consequently, when we locate our own power, we fear that it will lead us to repeat that destructive behaviour towards someone else. This fear of power and its confusion with tyranny seems to hold a lot of clients back from accessing the full voice during a Voice Movement Journey. It is therefore very important that the group leader addresses the issue of power and helps clients rescue it from its association with destructivity.

Just as there are emotions which arise before and during a Voice Movement Journey, the client is also usually left with the residue of particular emotions in the period following a journey which can be quite distressing.

One of the common feelings which clients disclose after taking a Voice Movement Journey is shame. During the journey, a client is able to expose and express things in sound which are normally kept hidden beneath the carefully constructed grammar of speech and gesture. Voice is a particularly raw and primal form of human expression and the act of vocalisation has an immediacy about it which can feel as if everything inside is passing up through the tube and out into the open. When the journey is over, there is therefore often a kind of hollow feeling, an emptiness generated by the expression. This has two sides. On the one hand, clients often feel relieved, purged and less burdened. On the other hand they can also feel deflated and depressed. Accompanying these feelings, clients may feel a sense of shame that they have exposed, revealed and spilled things which their mind tells them ought to remain within.

One of the ways to deal with these feelings in the aftermath of a Voice Movement Journey is to invite clients to share a key moment of their journey with the group. The group gathers in a circle and those clients who wish to share move into the centre of the circle and repeat a part of their journey. If the practitioner has been attentive, he or she ought to be able to select a moment from the client's journey and remind him of the body movement and vocal quality, giving the client a starting point.

Afterwards, the client discloses the negative feelings which she may have about her journey and the practitioner and group then enable the client to see the work from a positive point of view.

Singing Cure, Talking Cure

Many people choose to work therapeutically through a non-verbal strategy such as dance therapy or Voice Movement Therapy because they feel words do not get close enough to the root of their issues. They experience the limitations of the 'talking cure'. Yet, many clients also experience the down-side to the intensity of non-verbal work, which can provoke deep feelings in the body and the voice which have no name because they are being expressed but not described.

Often, in non-verbal therapy, it is destructive to seek to translate someone's therapeutic experience into words. Yet, there are other times when this is essential if clients are to be saved from a feeling of being isolated and overwhelmed by feelings which they cannot identify. Though speech is limiting, it has the advantage of being a shared language. When a feeling is named and spoken, the speaker has the comfort of knowing that most people in the room will have a good idea of what they are experiencing; and this makes the speaker feel connected and conjoined with others. With non-verbal work, however, if feelings always remain unnamed and unidentified, a client can feel isolated. Therefore, the practitioner must always ensure that room is created for discussion in the aftermath of something as intense as a Voice Movement Journey. At the same time, clients should always be afforded the right to leave the experience undiscussed.

CHAPTER 7

The Language of the Breath
The Mechanics of Breathing and its Influence on Mind and Body

The Act of Breathing

The process of breathing is tidal, continuous and spherical.

Like the tide, the breath undulates through an ebb and flow of inspiration and expiration which is ceaseless and life-long. Come rain or shine, in sickness and in health, breathing remains as a sign of life; and if it ceases for more than a few minutes, life is extinguished.

But, though the breath remains a constant aspect of physiological function, its nature is varied and each inspiration and expiration is toned with a quality which reveals a great deal about the psychological and physical state of the person who breathes.

On a psychological level, many emotional and instinctual sensations are revealed by and expressed through the breath: the huffs of fury, the puffs of rage, the sudden gasps of shock and the long open sighs of relief, the climactic breaths of orgasm and the constricted winds of exasperation. All that is felt is woven into the breath.

In Greek, the word for breath and the word for soul have the same root. In Latin, the words for soul and spirit originate in the word for wind. In fact, in many languages, air and soul come from the same root word. These linguistic connections remind us of the absolute essential nature of the breath as the vital food of the psyche.

The breath also reveals information about the physical state of an individual. In the breathing of some people, you can hear the crackling and popping of bronchial congestion; in others you can hear the desperate gasping of breath which may indicate a constricted airway; and in others, shallow and insubstantial breathing reveals muscle fatigue or paralysis.

Of course, the physical condition of the body influences the emotional sense of Self; and the feeling state of an individual in turn affects the sense of physical health. In the breath, it is possible to witness the intersection of the psychological and the physical; for the breath is as much an essential service to the body's organs and tissues as it is an emissary for psychological predicament.

The process of breathing is deeply affected by psychological state and in turn, mental predicament is influenced by the breath. Because of this consensual and cyclical influence, it is possible to influence psychological health positively by enhancing the process of breathing. By working on the breath we can break the vicious circle by which negative feelings lead to inhibited breathing which in turn compound and reinforce negative feelings.

However, in working on the breath we are also approaching a core somatic process and are, in consequence, also influencing physical function. Working with the breath is therefore a way of engaging at a fundamental level with a person's psychological and physical being through a process which is at once mental and physical. Moreover, the breath is an acoustic phenomenon and much of the information which is to be gleaned from the breath is perceived through listening rather than through looking. To understand the breath requires a sensitive ear that is attuned to the subtle musical contours of inspiration and expiration.

It is, of course, quite natural to respond to someone's gasps and sighs and to the overt expression of emotion which is communicated through respiratory sounds. Most people have the ability to detect the mood and ambience which underlies the sound of breathing. But to transpose the ear's sensitivity to breath into a therapeutic context requires a refining and honing of this ability.

Voice Movement Therapy comprises a systematic approach to working with the breath and the following is an outline of some of the aspects which constitute this approach.

To begin, it will be useful to identify and describe concisely the rudimentary mechanics, physiology and psychology of breathing.

The Mechanics of Breathing

The thorax, or thoracic cavity, which constitutes the upper half of the trunk, houses the lungs: two spongy, curvilinear, balloon-like organs which are composed of over three hundred million minuscule air sacs or alveoli (Figure 7.1). The blood, pumped by the semi-spherical heart, circulates through the

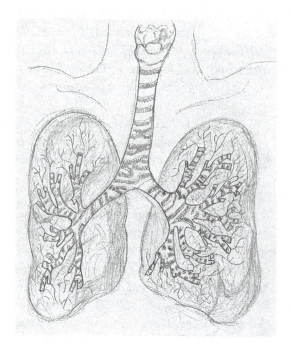

Figure 7.1

alveoli, absorbing oxygen from the air which is inspired from the external atmosphere and releasing carbon-dioxide which is expired into the same exterior environment. This oxygen which the blood absorbs is circulated throughout the body through a labyrinth of tubes and is released into all organs and tissue structures – which require it to function.

As a result of the inward passage of air through the respiratory pathway when we breathe in, the lungs inflate; and when we breathe out the lungs deflate and air is expelled. This process is crucial to the maintenance of life. If it ceases for more than four to five minutes, death is inevitable.

In order for the lungs to expand when we breathe in, increased volume has to be created in the torso, for when the lungs are inflated they occupy more space than when they are deflated; and this can be achieved in a number of ways.

The torso itself, like the respiratory tract, may be perceived as a cylinder or a large tube (Figure 7.2a). Consequently, in seeking to increase its volume to accommodate or instigate lung expansion there are, by the laws of geometry and mechanics, three motions which can be effected. First, the

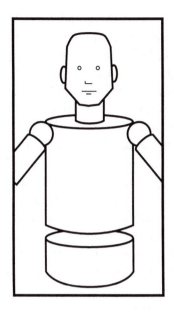

Figure 7.2a

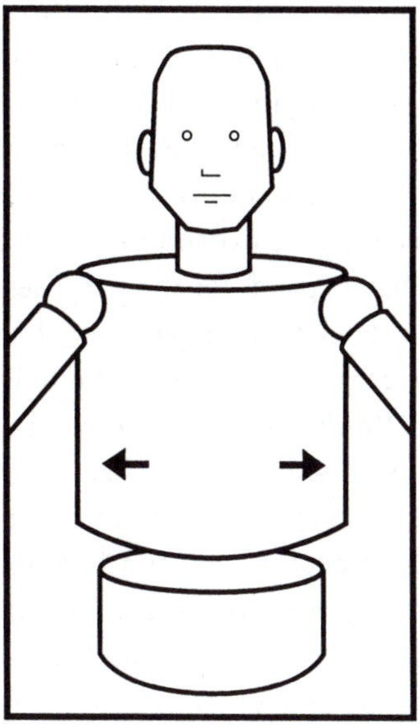

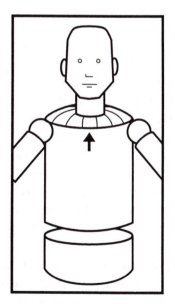

Figure 7.2b

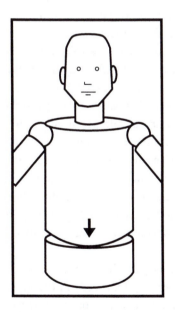

Figure 7.2c

Figure 7.2d

cylinder can be dilated to possess an increased diameter by expanding its walls outwards (Figure 7.2b). Second, the floor of the cylinder can be lowered, moving the base of the cylinder downwards, making it deeper from the bottom (Figure 7.2c). Third, the lid of the cylinder can be raised, moving the top of the cylinder upwards, making it higher from the top (Figure 7.2d).

In fact, these are the three mechanical and muscular means which the body employs to expand the torso, creating increased volume in which the lungs may expand, for the purposes of inspiration.

The diametrical expansion of the cylinder walls, often referred to as 'thoracic breathing', is achieved in the following way. The lungs are housed by a scaffolding of bones known as the rib cage which are curved in shape, ten pairs of which are attached to the back bone or vertebrae behind and to the breast bone or sternum at the front. The lower two pairs of ribs are shorter than the others and are attached only to the vertebrae with their other end protruding; these are known as the floating ribs. Although the top eight pairs of ribs are attached front and back, they are not fused solidly but are joined by cartilage and joints so as to be able to move.

Between the ribs, inside and outside the cage which they form, there are two sets of intercostal muscles, the expansion and contraction of which causes the ribs to be pulled upwards and outwards, increasing the size of the thoracic cavity. This causes the chest to rise and protrude at the front, back and sides creating a cylindrical dilation around the upper torso.

The lowering of the cylinder floor is achieved in the following way. Underneath the lungs there is a long muscle called the diaphragm which is stretched out from one side of the trunk to the other separating the thorax from the abdomen. When the diaphragm relaxes it bends upwards against the floor of the lungs, assuming a shape similar to an upside down salad bowl, decreasing thoracic space but increasing the volume of the abdomen. When it contracts, however, it is pulled downwards and flattened and because it is joined to a layer of tissue, known as the pleura, which is in turn joined to the floor of the lungs, it literally pulls the lungs down with it, expanding them from the bottom so that inspired air fills the freshly created space (Figure 7.3). When the diaphragm relaxes, it returns to its vertical curvature, assisting in the expulsion of air from the lungs.

Due to the laws of gravity and the morphological distribution of the air sacs or alveoli, there is a greater concentration of blood cells in the lower portion of the lungs. Consequently, the most efficient absorption of oxygen can occur when fresh inspired air finds its way to the bottom of the lungs.

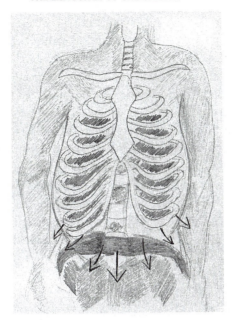

Figure 7.3

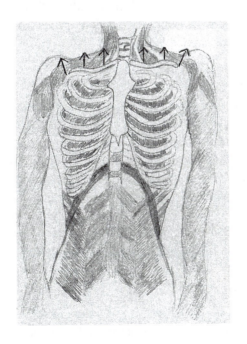

Figure 7.4

This is the main reason why maximum displacement of the diaphragm during breathing, often referred to as 'diaphragmatic breathing', is believed by some to be most advantageous to health. This displacement of the diaphragm is the method of expansion and contraction which infants spontaneously employ to breathe until they have learned to effect the dilation of the torso walls.

During optimal breathing the movement of the diaphragm occurs in tandem with intercostal muscle motility, simultaneously expanding and contracting the cylindrical walls of the torso and lowering and raising the diaphragmatic floor by which the entire torso is inflated and deflated.

The raising of the cylinder's roof is achieved by muscular contraction across the top of the back and shoulders which has the effect of elevating the clavicles, or collar bones, creating increased space around the top of the lungs (Figure 7.4). This method of expansion, often referred to as 'clavicular breathing', is frequently employed in the service of exercise or extreme activity when extra quantities of air are required.

The distribution of muscular displacement or palpable movement of the body in these three areas of chest, abdomen and the clavicular region constitute part of what we may call the Breathing Pattern, which may be more or less in service of optimal functioning. I shall now outline the components of the Breathing Pattern.

Breathing Pattern Component One: Muscular Displacement

The first component dimension to a Breathing Pattern is therefore the distribution of what we shall call Muscular Displacement, that is the observable or palpable muscle action accompanying respiration and its distribution across the torso, which may show greater or lesser motility around the chest and the back to achieve diametrical expansion of the torso's walls; may show greater or lesser movement in the muscles of the abdominal wall, revealing the motion of the diaphragm which expands the floor of the cylindrical torso downwards; and may show greater or lesser muscle action across the shoulders to raise the clavicles and expand the torso upwards.

Breathing Pattern Component Two: Force and Pressure

In addition to the expandability, elasticity or degree of displacement in the muscles of the torso which assist inspiration, this musculature also acts within a certain spectrum of force or pressure by which it decreases the internal volume of the thorax assisting the deflation of the lungs and the expiration of breath. In assessing the way in which someone breathes we may therefore observe the power, force, pressure or strength with which the respiratory musculature compresses and contracts the body. This is turn increases the pressure with which air in the respiratory tract travels towards the vocal cords with the effect of drawing the cords together under greater force and thus creating a louder sound.

The second component to the Breathing Pattern is therefore the contractile force in the muscles responsible for expiration.

Breathing Pattern Component Three: Respiratory Frequency

Naturally, respiration takes place in time and therefore within a continuum between faster and slower. The third component to the Breathing Pattern is therefore the amount of respiratory cycles, or combined inspirations and expirations, which take place in a given unit of time.

Breathing Pattern Component Four: Tidal Volume

The combination of these three aforementioned dimensions to the Breathing Pattern naturally influence the quantity of air that is exchanged with each respiratory cycle. This amount of air breathed may therefore be identified as a fourth dimension to the Breathing Pattern and may be defined as the volume of air which passes into the lungs with each inspiration and out of the lungs with each expiration. This may be called the tidal volume of air and the quantity of air which a person is able to exchange may be called their tidal capacity.

Breathing Pattern Component Five: Sensation of Depth and Shallowness

The Breathing Pattern is also composed of what is often described as the degree of depth or shallowness which a person experiences during the breathing process. For the most part, the depth or shallowness of breathing is a subjective sensation arising from the combination of the other dimensions. For example, fast respiratory frequency combined with maximum thoracic displacement, a degree of clavicular displacement and minimal abdominal movement would create the sensation of shallowness. Low respiratory frequency combined with enhanced abdominal displacement would, conversely, create the sensation of depth. This subjective sensation is underpinned by the objective depth to which the inspired air in the lungs descends. Because increased amplitude or displacement of the diaphragm pulls the tissue floor of the lungs downwards, drawing air deeply into the lungs, it creates a sensation of depth greater than that experienced with minimal diaphragmatic movement and increased thoracic expansion, which tends to concentrate the exchange of air at the top of the lungs.

The positive sense which many people derive from abdominal displacement may therefore be due to the ability of the body to sense that more efficient gaseous exchange takes place in the lower regions of the lungs.

Breathing Pattern Component Six: Dimensions of the Upper Airway

The stream of breath which is inspired and expired passes through a tube or tract which dilates and constricts, lengthens and shortens; and during vocalisation, this gives rise to distinct timbres. However, the dimensions of the upper respiratory tract also affect the experience of breathing. For example, when we blow someone a kiss or cool down hot food, the airway is narrow and short, that is in Flute Configuration. When we steam up a pair of spectacles to clean them, the airway is more dilated and lengthened, that is in Clarinet Configuration. If we then open the oral and pharyngeal cavities, lower the larynx and yawn, the tract is in Saxophone Configuration.

The sixth component dimension to the Breathing Pattern is therefore the configuration of the upper respiratory tract or tube which is identical with the vocal tract.

The Effect of the Breathing Pattern on Mind and Body

By comprehending the process of breathing in simple terms as being made up of these six components, it is possible to both empathise with and to understand some of the commonly occurring and different patterns of breathing. It also provides the foundations for understanding the way that certain patterns of breathing affect the psyche in particular ways.

For example, a driven passage of air expelled from the lungs during expiration may be maintained at constant pressure by consistent contractile muscle action, but if the tube through which this air passes is dilated and constricted it will decrease and increase the pressure respectively. Therefore, the smaller the diameter of the airway, the greater the sensation of air pressure in the tube when the amount and force of air expelled from the lungs remains constant. Many people, as a result of habitual muscle use, have a narrow tract with a particularly squeezed pharyngeal space. If such clients also have a large lung capacity with breath expelled under high pressure due to strong contractile force of the respiratory musculature, there is an enormous pressure of breath which has to be bottle-necked through a very small opening. Such a client may have the sensation of breath being damned up under great force and consequently may feel emotionally pent up and pressurised, about to burst, forever waiting release but never able to express or depress the pressure.

When someone feels exasperated or furious and would like to shout but is refrained by the circumstances, it is common to make a Flute Configuration and blow air through its narrow dimensions; people also often suck air in audibly through a flute-shaped vocal tract when expecting bad news or experiencing sustained suspense. The experience of shallowness is also often instigated by a narrow and short tube through which a limited volume of tidal air can pass, whilst depth can be facilitated by increased tube dimensions. Conversely, the same contractile muscle power expelling air from the lungs through a tract which is dilated and lengthened so that a greater volume of air passes out in a given unit of time can create the sensation of slippage, a lack of control or depleted containment and a sense of not being able to store or restore any breath and therefore energy.

From time to time, most people experience a moment of such anticipation and heightened expectation that they will, literally, hold their breath. This holding, which is a cessation of the entire breathing process, also has the effect of putting feelings on hold. It as though the holding of the breath suspends emotions in mid-air until it is known which way the wind blows and which way fate has fallen. At the crescendo of such moments, if things turn out well, the breath is released in a sigh of joy and relief which is audible in the sound of the expiration. If things turn out ill, then this too is detectable in the released breath of depression and disappointment.

In my experience, however, some people habitually hold their breath momentarily between the inspiration and the expiration. Rather than a continuous and cyclical waxing and waning where inspiration slips immediately and fluidly into expiration there is rather a pause, a suspension, a minute version of the kind of holding we would expect in times of extreme anticipation.

These examples are a sample of some psychosomatic patterns of breathing by which emotional experience and respiratory action interrelate and influence one another.

Practical Method: Enhancing the Breathing Pattern

By recognising the way the Breathing Pattern affects the psyche we can effect positive changes to psychological experience through working directly on the physical mechanics of breathing.

The work on breath which constitutes part of the Voice Movement Therapy methodology consists of a series of exercises and guided experiential processes which enables the client to become conscious of the components of their Breathing Pattern and make changes to their employment which facilitate physical and psychological well-being.

To enable the client to experience potential for the three areas of displacement, the practitioner places his hands over the relevant areas and, utilising a little pressure, amplifies and exaggerates the natural movement of the appropriate muscles, increasing the sensation of natural motility. By varying the amount of pressure which the practitioner uses, the client can

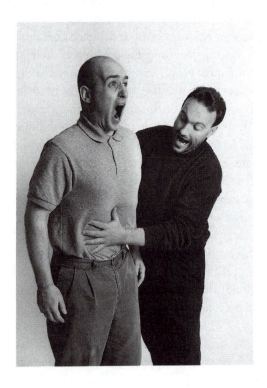

Photograph 7.1

experience a spectral range of contractile and expiratory pressures and where there is muscle damage, fatigue or disability, alternative muscle groups can be trained to assume the contractile work. Usually, the practitioner works with specific focus on the three areas of displacement: the area of the central torso and rib cage; the abdominal area (Photograph 7.1); and the upper chest and clavicular area.

Further to this, the aim of the work is to facilitate an experience of the tube and a sense of its elasticity. To this end, the practitioner encourages clients to experience its potential for dilation and contraction and for lengthening and shortening by which they are enabled to acquire an increased malleability of the tube, thereby enhancing respiratory sensation.

During the process of investigation and intervention, the practitioner observes the volume of air that is exchanged and the frequency with which cycles of inspiration and expiration occur, encouraging component combinations which facilitate optimal functioning and a positive sense of well-being.

Amplified Sensation

It is useful to remember that one of the effects of the breath upon the body is that of amplification. In other words, breathing induces sensation. Therefore, enhanced breathing has the effect of intensifying sensation.

The process of breathing serves the process of respiration which infuses the blood with oxygen which is then carried and delivered to all the organs and tissue structures of the body. In order to understand the nature of breath work, it must be appreciated that because breathing oxygenates all body parts it therefore has the capacity to increase sensation throughout the somatic container. Often, during enhanced breathing, a niggling ache will become an excruciating pain and a slightly stiff neck, for example, will become extreme hyperkinetic rigidity. Facilitating change in the pattern of breathing may therefore stimulate unpleasant sensations within the body as well as providing the means to establishing greater comfort and ease. For, oxygen is like a sense enhancer which magnifies and amplifies that which is already there.

A restricted Breathing Pattern which keeps tidal air flow to a minimum and ensures that the breath remains shallow will inevitably deplete sensation. For someone experiencing pain or discomfort the restricted Breathing Pattern consequently pays the short-term reward of anaesthetising negative sensations. Very often, clients with a depleted respiratory activity have a localised somatic discomfort: a pain in the back or limbs, a stiff neck, uncomfortable joints, residual pain from previous injury or internal pain resulting from disease or malfunction of an organ. Such clients may have discovered, often quite unconsciously, that by restricting the intensity of oxygenation, they remain less aware of the painful parts of the body.

When clients with such physical discomfort are encouraged to increase the depth of breathing and to extend the tidal air flow, very often the initial experience is of increased discomfort in the affected parts of the body. This can cause some distress as it is as though the injured or dysfunctional part of the body were being made worse by the breath work rather than better. Unfortunately, this is often a necessary stage through which to pass on the way to recovery and further relief from pain; and it is necessary for both practitioner and client to understand the long-term sacrifice which is made in return for the short-term relief gained by a restricted and inhibited Breathing Pattern.

We cannot control the distribution of oxygen to the various parts of the body. Therefore, if we restrict the process of oxygenation in order to deplete sensation in one painful part of the body, we will inevitably inhibit the entire respiratory process and the delivery of oxygen to all parts of the body. Consequently, the tissue, muscle and organs of the entire body cannot work at optimal functioning. Furthermore, although an inhibited Breathing Pattern may restrict discomfort in an injured part of the body, it also depletes the opportunity for that injury to recover fully because respiration is so vital to the process by which tissue is nourished. If a client can be patient and trust that short-term intensification of discomfort will give way to a more complete painlessness, then enhancing the Breathing Pattern can do two things. It can encourage damaged tissue to mend and it can return a healthy respiratory process of oxygenation to the rest of the body.

In addition to experiencing amplified physical sensation, clients will often also experience increased emotional sensation, volatility and animation. The client's expression of emotion will often emerge through the sounds arising from the audible breath. Gasps, sobs, shivers, exasperations, exultant jubilations, melancholy whimpers and a whole spectrum of feelings may be heard within the breath sounds. At all times it is vital that the practitioner affirms, encourages and supports the client with an open heart and an objective mind. Providing the practitioner is well trained, combining this hands-on manipulative work with vocal investigations can enable the tonal and timbral range of the client's voice to be remarkably increased, providing the means for a more complete expression of the psyche in sound.

Breath Work and Massage

The best way to conduct breath work with a client who has localised bodily pain or discomfort is to combine the breathing work with massage of the affected bodily area. This requires dexterous and careful use of the hands which need to divide their time between enhancing the Breathing Pattern and massaging restricted areas.

Within the therapeutic field, many of the manipulatory and massage-based techniques are employed quite separately and often by different practitioners from those utilising dance and expressive movement. Moreover, attendance to the client's vocalisation is rarely incorporated into either of these two approaches. In the massage modality which descends from the Swedish tradition and in manipulatory therapies such as osteopathy, physiotherapy and chiropractic, the silent client is usually passive, often lying on a table where she is mobilised by the practitioner. In expressive movement, such as dance movement therapy, meanwhile, the silent client is often untouched by the practitioner and is free to explore their own movement patterns before an analytic and interpretive witness. Both approaches, naturally, have different uses and provide equally necessary services for diverse problems. However, the separation of the two approaches also denies clients of the benefits of an integrated approach. Voice Movement Therapy seeks to synthesise tenets of expressive movement with those of massage and manipulation in combination with vocalisation. I have called this strategy Voice Movement Massage.

Practical Method: Voice Movement Massage

In Voice Movement Massage the client moves according to an expressive dance, authenticating their own impulses and experiences artistically. At the same time, the practitioner maintains physical contact with the client, moving as an improvisational dance partner whilst simultaneously massaging and manipulating the body, releasing tension in areas where excess stress is apparent, softening tissue where excess solidity can be felt and enhancing sensation of the Breathing Pattern and method of voice production.

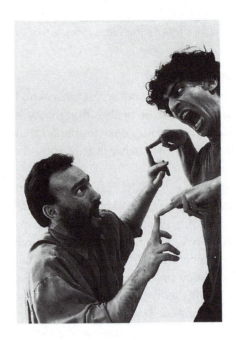

Photograph 7.2

Photograph 7.3

During this process, the client is leader of the dance and can depart from contact or move towards the practitioner or otherwise influence the spatial and physical relationship with him at any time. This technique enables the practitioner to respond to the body as it is in motion, building a picture of the skeletal distribution of tension based on a direct experience of kinetic expression. Furthermore, because the client's dance is rooted in the experience and expression of feeling, the respiratory pattern as well as the voice paints a collage within which is revealed an emotionality that in some way contributes to the body's muscular state. Voice Movement Massage develops naturally out of the work on Breathing Enhancement. At first, the practitioner's contact with the client is through hand contact with the torso. As the rapport unfolds, the practitioner gradually uses more and more of his own body to guide the physical journey of the client. Within the Voice Movement Massage, therefore, contact between the two persons may range from something as tiny as fingertips to fingertips (Photograph 7.2), through to motions of carrying in the arms, to motions in which the practitioner may use his entire body as a platform of support for the client (Photograph 7.3).

This technique of Voice Movement Massage involves attendance to specific parts of the body which relate to the process of breathing and voice production, the most significant of which are the neck, the chest and the abdomen.

The Neck

The neck is the host of that mysterious area called the throat which for many is the locus of conflict and ambivalence. It seems as if the throat is like a bottle-neck and a point of convergence for two pathways: one being the flow of cognitive thoughts which, in terms of somatic sensation feel as though they descend from the head to be expelled from the mouth as words; the other being the flow of feelings which feel as though they rise up from the heart and the belly to emerge from the mouth as unformed sounds. For some people, these two pathways are incongruent or in conflict and the thoughts which descend from the head act to critically suppress the feelings which rise from the depths. Consequently, there is a war in the neck which neither party wins and which culminates in a numbing of feeling and thought ending in silence.

In facilitating the breach of this silence and encouraging free vocalisation, a common problem is one of unpleasant physical sensations in the neck, or more specifically the throat, which seem to somatise that inner part of the

Photograph 7.4

client which is determined not to let the voice out. It is therefore not uncommon for a client to cough or gag, placing her hands around the neck and describing a feeling of constriction. The dimension of the vocal tract in such a situation is normally short and narrow and the voice quality is usually therefore Flute Timbre. In order to enable the client to overcome this suppression of the voice and to expand the expressive range, it is necessary to encourage the vocal tract to lengthen and dilate, moving firstly into Clarinet and then into the Saxophone Configuration. The purpose of aiming to fully lengthen and dilate into Saxophone is that it prevents the constriction of the tissue structures which can cause friction between the vocal folds; at the same time, it keeps the voice tube open so that the sound can be amplified rather than dampened or quashed.

One way to achieve this is through direct massage and manipulation by which the practitioner takes hold of the client's larynx encouraging it to move vertically up and down (Photograph 7.4). Careful manipulation of the larynx in the neck frees it from the constraints of solidified connective tissue, increasing malleability in the laryngeal musculature, facilitating the ability to lower the floor of the vocal tract and thus increasing timbral resonance. Naturally, in the hands of an incompetent practitioner, or for certain clients with heightened sensitivity to the connotations of contact with the neck, this can provoke fears of being throttled or strangled. The practitioner must have been trained to know exactly where to place the fingers and how much pressure to use; the muscles of this region are attached to a freely suspended hyoid bone which can easily be broken, and indeed is usually snapped when someone is strangled. Furthermore, there are some clients for whom this way of working is entirely inappropriate.

As the practitioner massages the neck, he can begin to work across the shoulder and down to the scapulas, meeting the area which is worked on through contact with the chest.

The Chest

Contact with the chest enables the practitioner to positively enhance modes of movement and the Breathing Pattern and thus the efficacy of voice production and the respiratory processes. Like most of the physical movement investigations which constitute Voice Movement Therapy, this operates around a spherical conception of space which moves the body through convex and concave configurations. To begin, the practitioner places one hand in the centre of the torso, just below the sternum, and the other hand in the middle of the back. Using pressure alternately between the two hands, the client is moved back and forth between a position in which the spine is curled forwards creating a concave implosion at the front and a convex curve at the back of the body and a position in which the spine is arched back forming a concave curve at the back and a convex arch at the front. During these movements, the practitioner uses manipulation to elongate and stretch the spine, discouraging vertebral compression. As the pendulum-like movements proceed, the practitioner combines manipulative pressure and massage so as to assist in the liberation of the Breathing Pattern from ineffective habitual activity.

One of the areas which, when expanded and released from compressive solidification, can assist an expanded respiratory capacity is the space beneath the scapulas. By working the hands under the shoulder bone and massaging the tissue therein, the client can experience an increase in

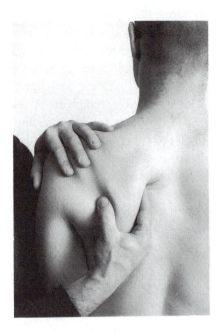

Photograph 7.5

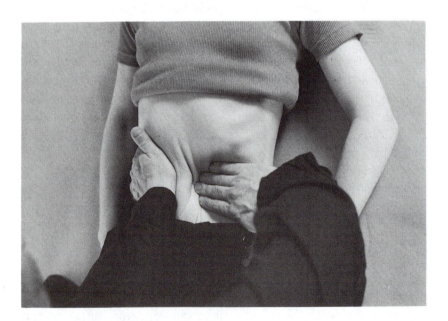

Photograph 7.6

magnitude and breathing volume as well as feeling released from tension (Photograph 7.5).

The Abdomen

When the diaphragm moves downwards, it puts pressure on the abdominal organs instigating a gentle squeeze or compression of the blood vessels serving to increase circulation. This is a positive force up to a certain limit and excess pressure on the organs is prevented by the expansion of the abdominal wall which displaces outwards to form an unfashionable but essential paunch or belly, re-establishing the space for the abdominal contents. If the muscles of this wall are too taut, however, such displacement is hindered and optimal lung expansion depleted. Through Voice Movement Massage, the practitioner can enable the client to release the abdominal wall from excess tension and facilitate enhanced breathing (Photograph 7.6).

When the practitioner makes physical contact with the abdominal area it highlights the psychophysical relationship between the vocal tract and the stomach and bowels. The mouth and the oro-pharynx are multi-functional, serving as the respiratory tract through which gas passes during breathing, the digestive tract through which food is ingested and vomited and the vocal tract out of which sounds emerge. In the brain, neurological pathways are organised to mirror the spatial organisation of the body. That is to say that two parts of the body which are in close spatial proximity, such as the nose and lips, have their nerve endings close together in the brain. The region of the pharynx and larynx is highly innervated with nerves and the various constituting structures are so close together that it is almost impossible for the brain to distinguish between sensations of the upper trachea and sensations which emanate from the oesophagus. Consequently, any uncomfortable sensation in that region becomes generalised as a sensation in 'the throat'. Furthermore, because of the close proximity of the oesophagus and the trachea and because the same tract serves to accommodate food and voice, sensations or sensory memories associated with one can become equated with the other. In therapeutic work, this is commonly observed when a client is attempting to open the vocal tract to its widest gauge, that is to Saxophone Configuration. During such a process, physical sensations and emotional experiences connected to digestion and therefore to intestinal processes can be vivified which often tends to cause the client to silence herself for fear of regurgitating intestinal contents.

Indeed, there is widespread occurrence of psychogenic selective mutism in combination with eating problems which is particularly prevalent in children. Selective mutism denotes a syndrome in which a client refrains from vocalising in specific contexts whilst resuming voice in others. Mutism often occurs in combination with anorexia or can occur in the aftermath of vomiting following the intake of food. The potential therapeutic value of Voice Movement Therapy has been applied in work with women suffering from eating disorders by psychotherapist and musician Irene Kessler in Florida, USA as part of her doctoral research (Kessler 1997). By using vocal sound, focusing particularly on the movement of the voice tube in the body, clients were able to investigate their relationship to eating and resolve negative and self-destructive habits.

Contact with the abdomen also stimulates in the client the sensation of the stomach as a seat of primary affects, a notion which is found in many cultures worldwide and which for centuries has been part of the vernacular vocabulary in many European languages, which are full of metaphors pointing to the stomach as an emotional centre. For example, the abdomen is the reservoir of the deeper, less frequently accessed emotions such as grief. Rarely do we reach to touch our chest when in bereavement; frequently the hands clutch the abdominal cavity which is often experienced not as a compartmentalised composition of intestines, bladder, stomach, liver and womb but as a single mass of psychophysical experience which we may call the belly.

The belly is also the seat of our deepest laughter, the belly laugh. It is not the giggles of a heart in love, but the guttural roar of extreme humour. The belly is also a container for our wisdom, all of those insights which we have acquired as a result of experience and which formulate the things we know instinctively down in the belly: our gut instincts. The belly as a combined container for laughter and wisdom is deliciously symbolised in the great laughing Buddha.

Over-Breathing or Hyperventilation

During any kind of work on the breath, one of the dangers which the practitioner must guard against is leading the client to hyperventilate. Hyperventilation means over-breathing. It usually occurs when a person increases the amount of air inspired in a given amount of time, usually measured in litres per minute. As a result of over-breathing, too much oxygen is absorbed and too much carbon dioxide is released, consequently, carbon dioxide levels in the blood start to drop, upsetting its acid-alkaline base.

Lowered levels of carbon dioxide in the blood strengthen the bond between haemoglobin and oxygen making it more difficult for the haemoglobin to give the oxygen up to the tissue of the brain and other organs which need it. This state, called hypoxia, can cause increased pressure in the arteries, known as hypertension. In addition, the lowered oxygen level in tissue cells results in a lowered level of oxygen in the veins which leads to dilation of the venous blood vessels which can in turn cause varicose veins and haemorrhoids. The sufferer is also likely to experience exhaustion, tiredness, and increased heart rate and there can occur a cut in oxygen rate to the brain of up to 50 per cent. Now, caught in a vicious Catch 22, the brain's response to this condition is to stimulate and excite the breathing mechanism even more which further increases the over-breathing, leading to a progressive reduction of carbon dioxide. The body, though, has various mechanisms of defence against the loss of carbon dioxide which include spasm of the bronchi and blood vessels, increased levels of cholesterol production in the liver and lowering of the arterial pressure. However, this in turn causes hypotension, increased mucus and phlegm production, increased production of lactic acid and in consequence causes metabolism to suffer.

Because the respiratory process serves to oxygenate all tissue, not a single part of the body is exempt from the potential problems resulting from hyperventilation. In fact, people with Hyperventilation Syndrome are frequently misdiagnosed as having a variety of disorders including Multiple Sclerosis, peripheral neuropathy, epilepsy and mental illness.

The decreased carbon dioxide levels which mark the onset of hyperventilation in combination with the body's defence against it affect the central neurovascular system, causing faintness, dizziness, unsteadiness, impairment of concentration and memory, feelings of unreality and, sometimes, loss of consciousness. They affect the peripheral neurovascular pathways causing numbness, coldness of the fingers and toes and tingling in the limbs and face. They affect the skeletal muscles causing tremors and spasms. They affect the respiratory system causing shortness of breath, tightness in the chest and affects the heart, causing palpitations.

During hyperventilation, a variable degree of slowing in the frequency of the brain waves occurs which correlates with alterations in the level of consciousness. When mean electroencephalographic frequency falls below 5 cycles per second, conscious awareness is markedly reduced. Of course, the body, being innately wise, takes advantage of this lack of consciousness and returns to a more normal breathing rate. However, if hyperventilation is immediately reinstated, the person swings back and forth between different brain wave frequencies, the overall effect being one of an ecstatic state; for it is indeed an altered state of consciousness.

Despite the fact that some approaches to therapeutic work deliberately induce states of hyperventilation, claiming that it offers an opportunity to explore the psyche from a heightened perspective, I do not endorse such practices. At all times the client should feel clear-headed, capable of feeling sensation throughout the skeletal musculature, and clients should be able to breathe at a regular even pace using all areas of expansion. If a client begins to feel dizzy and starts to hyperventilate, the breathing rate should be slowed down and the client should be encouraged to breathe evenly with maximum abdominal displacement. There is no advantage to be gained by encouraging the client to breathe themselves into a frenzied and agitated state.

The Nature of Asthma

The most widespread and common respiratory condition suffered by people from all walks of life is asthma; and though this book is focused primarily on psychological difficulties, it will be useful to approach the subject here because it is an example of a somatic condition which responds well to a psychophysical therapeutic approach – because the condition is often related to psychological issues.

The term 'asthma' is used as an umbrella word to cover a variety of conditions which have in common intermittent periods of breathlessness. This breathlessness is caused by periodic narrowing of the bronchial tubes or airways inside the lung. Many people experience the onset of an asthmatic period as an 'attack' and there are many factors which can trigger an asthma attack.

Because of the broad range of factors which cause asthma and the spectrum of effects which asthma can have on the airways, it is not easy to provide a simple definition of asthma.

However, the main symptoms of asthma are wheeze, breathlessness, cough and chest tightness and the basic principle is this: asthma is a condition in which the airways or tubes within the lung become inflamed. This inflammation makes them more sensitive to the 'triggers' that cause airways to narrow, reducing the amount of air that can flow through them. This reduction in air flow makes the person breathless and often makes them sound 'wheezy'. The common term for these highly sensitive airways is 'twitchy tubes', though the medical term is 'bronchial hyper-reactivity'. The medical opinion is that asthma effects people in such a variety of ways that any treatment needs to be personalised to respond to the unique disposition of the sufferer.

Asthma is an important condition to consider from a therapeutic point of view because it is so common. Around 15 per cent of primary school aged children and around 7 per cent of the general population in the UK suffer from asthma. It is also a condition which has increased over the last 20 years. Currently, it is estimated that over three million individuals in England and Wales alone have asthma.

There is certainly a hereditary component to asthma but there are also environmental factors known to be responsible for causing it. Allergens, cigarette smoke and the house dust mite, pollution, exercise, fumes and odours as well as emotional stress are all known triggers. Asthma can also be brought on by a cold or a viral infection.

Amongst children, the house dust mite is the most common trigger. When someone is exposed to the faeces of a mite over a period of time the white cells become sensitive to it and as it is inhaled, the lining of the bronchial tubes react to it, becoming inflamed. This inflammation makes the lining very sensitive so that any other trigger will result in the narrowing of the tubes.

The main cause of the constriction which causes the breathlessness in asthma is inflammation. The airway is lined with a delicate protective layer made up of different cells. Some of these cells produce mucus while others clear the mucus away by moving it up the bronchial tubes with tiny fingers found on the surface of the cells. In asthma, these fingers are prevented from doing their job properly.

When a trigger is inhaled, like a mite, a pollen seed, cigarette smoke or other irritant, three things happen to this cellular lining. First, one of the layers becomes swollen. Second, the mucus cells produce more mucus, which has to be coughed up to clear the airways. Third, the muscle wall of the tubes contracts. The result of these three actions is that the airways narrow, making it difficult to get air in and out.

There are a number of drugs used to alleviate asthma; and there are two main kinds. First, there are the 'relievers' which relax the muscle walls of the airways allowing them to dilate so that air can get in and out more easily. These drugs are knows as 'bronchodilators' and are usually inhaled with an inhaler. Second, there are 'preventers' which reduce the inflammation in the airways. Unlike inhaled bronchodilators – which are taken at the onset of an attack – preventers are taken on a regular basis, usually twice a day.

One of the ways a client can keep in touch with the state of his airways is through the use of a simple device called a 'peak flow meter'. This is a simple and cheap device which measures the maximum or peak rate at which air can be expelled from the lungs. The peak flow meter is a small tube with a moving cursor inside a meter at the side. The client checks that the cursor is on zero, takes a deep breath in, places the meter in the mouth, closes the lips and blows suddenly and hard. They then record the number registered by the cursor. This enables clients with asthma to measure the effectiveness of their treatment and management plan.

Because of the underlying causes of asthma, anything which encourages the smooth muscle of the airways to relax and the inner lining of the airways to dilate will assist in decreasing the frequency of asthma attacks and the severity of one when it occurs.

Because so much of the imagery which underpins Voice Movement Therapy is focused on the idea of expanding tubes, it has a very positive and relieving effect on those suffering from asthma. The client is encouraged to take the idea of the expanding voice tube and extend this sensation to the feeling throughout the chest, imagining that all the tubes in the lungs are expanding. Though this is no substitute for an existing traditional management plan, the power of imagery is certainly potent enough to make a significant positive contribution.

Case Study: Martha

Managing Asthma and Climbing Mountains

Martha had suffered a severe spinal injury in a road traffic accident which had left her paralysed in both legs and one arm, blind in one eye and permanently scarred across her face. The accident occurred when she was 36 years old; she was 43 when she came to work with me. At the time of the accident she lived with her husband, who had since divorced her, and their two children who had since gone to live with Martha's sister.

Martha had suffered from asthma since childhood and on occasions the attacks, from which she still suffered, would cause her to experience muscle spasm throughout the torso, instigate blurred vision in her healthy eye and leave her feeling exhausted.

Before I even began working with Martha my attention was drawn to her propriety and sense of correctness. In her discussion with me during the initial taking of her history she was polite, punctilious with detail, succinct and extremely perceptive. I was also struck by the way she dressed: tightly fitting blouse, jacket and trousers.

On my asking Martha to create a sense of a containing sphere she proceeded to steer herself in her wheelchair, tracing an area only slightly larger than herself and I could not help feeling that she had made something to hem her in the same way as she seemed to be hemmed into her clothes, her wheelchair and her manner of discourse.

On introducing Martha to some physical movements involving guiding the torso back and forth from convex to concave, I pointed out to her that the Spherical Space which she had created was not big enough to accommodate her in stretching her arms out. Having made a larger sphere, Martha began to pursue the physical exercises with enthusiasm. However, now that she was animated it was clear to me that her clothing also restricted her movement; so, at my suggestion we loosened the top button of her blouse, took off her jacket and adjusted the belt that passed around her waist and strapped her into the chair. As she did this she said that she had trouble keeping herself in her wheelchair because if she stooped forwards she did not have the muscular strength to stop herself from falling out of the chair completely. I said that it seemed ironic that she should be strapped into a chair, given that after the accident the seat belt had entwined about her neck and kept her from escaping the wreckage until the emergency team had cut her out.

When we came to explore the Breathing Pattern it seemed logical to imagine that her internal experience was comparable to her sense of a compressing and stifling outer space which kept her strapped in with no room to move. Indeed, in listening to the breath, it appeared that the vocal tract was quite tightly constricted in the Flute Configuration and the morphology of her tissue around the neck and shoulders seemed extremely dense and tightly packed to the touch. I therefore suggested to Martha that we attempt to do the same with the inner tubes as we had done with her outer sphere and enlarge them. I thus began to massage her neck and shoulders whilst simultaneously guiding her with gentle pressure through spherical movements. I asked Martha to imagine that she had large tubes running throughout her body which carried breath to all her muscles and that the main tube ran from her lips down her torso. Now, I began teaching her how to lengthen and dilate the vocal tract to the Saxophone Configuration. At one point she stopped and looked a little worried and said: 'I keep expecting that I am going to have a spasm but I don't think I am'.

As a result of this work, Martha began to feel that she was gaining 'room to move' as well as 'room to breathe'. Now she wanted to find her voice.

Martha had been aphasic, that is unable to speak, for nearly a year following the accident. Indeed, it is common for major shock to silence the voice. A short period of speech therapy had enabled her to refind her voice, but on rediscovering it she experienced it to be 'extremely frail'. To my ears, her voice was in Clarinet, high in pitch with a great amount of free air with a very limited range of prosody.

During the Voice Movement Therapy work, however, I observed that though predominantly quiet and softened by a high degree of free air, her voice seemed to switch spontaneously into low-pitched intense growls which lasted only momentarily. Second, the fingers of her active hand seemed to be making repetitive and rhythmical gripping movements causing an alternating hypertension and relaxation throughout the entire torso. I began working with this by asking her to amplify, exaggerate and intensify both the vocal switches between high, light, soft, airy, wispy sounds and low, guttural, intense growling sounds as well as the physical switches between tense gripping movements and released relaxation of the fingers. As she proceeded to rehearse this instruction I began to imagine her to be climbing a mountain and suggested that she try to use this image to give specificity and substance to her work. Her reply, to my surprise and amusement, was that prior to the accident, one of her hobbies had been rock-climbing.

As we worked the scenario, I suggested that she imagine that the softer sounds were satisfied gasps and sighs of satisfaction as she reached various resting plateaus during the ascent of the mountain and that the lower more assertive sounds were ambitious and driven sounds of toil and determination accompanying the difficult and effortful climb. As she rehearsed, her body and voice took on epic proportion, her muscles bulged and her vocal sounds swung and sang. As I watched and listened my eyes and ears saw and heard a multitude of images which I relayed to Martha in words as she worked: I witnessed and described an ape, a savage Neanderthal, a grumbling bear, a giant, an avid explorer, a prowling leopard, a great bovine, part buffalo part mule – and as I spoke and she worked I felt a certain increase in her aggressive instincts radiate from this quiet and morose woman.

Seeking to enable the client to sense her aggression in a creative framework I guided her through an imaginary journey where she conceived of herself as a prehistoric mythical creature, part leopard, part bear and part bull. The driving force for this animal's movement was extreme hunger and her actions were hindered by an injury, a wound. I asked Martha to experience the fateful combination of hunger, anger and extreme vulnerability due to injury. The sounds which she released were both terrifying and tear-provoking as her body clamoured and careened.

It should be remembered that people who have been disabled are not hindered in their dreams, but run, jump, twist and turn unimpeded by the damaged frame which they confront when the waking hour comes. In exploring the Self through voice and movement, disabled people can capitalise on the dream time by exploring the able and unimpeded body of the dream through the vocal and choreographic waking imagination.

All the time during my work with Martha I was in close physical contact with her, helping her feel safe enough and secure enough to know that she would not fall out of the chair and hurt herself yet free enough within the chair fully to investigate the journey. I held her around the abdomen, hugged her shoulders, sat on one arm of the wheelchair with one ankle on each of the foot rests as we danced together in intimate yet task-orientated proximity. Then I noticed her eyes; they were closed.

On asking Martha to speak a little of her sight she explained that her sight had always been poor, even as a child, but mentioned that when mountaineering she rarely wore glasses but did most of the work 'by feel'; she would only put her glasses on when she stopped and wanted to view the landscape. I therefore suggested that she now remove the glasses which she still wore in order to assist the eye that had not been blinded in the accident and continue to rehearse. When she took them off I could sense the fabric of her vulnerability; indeed, the off-centre and asymmetrical set of her eyes to me gave Martha the appearance of timidity and defencelessness. However, the moment she began again the choreographic gripping and the vocal transformations her eyes became electrified, deliberate, concentrated and bold as she became totally absorbed in the climb. It was then that for some reason I thought of the Cyclops, the mythical one-eyed giant who captured Jason and his crew. I suggested the image of the Cyclops to this now energised woman who seemed to be discovering such vitality and potency through the work and she placed herself at the opening of a great cave and she began jumping up and down in the chair and calling, yodelling and booming. As the session proceeded her body became more animated and her voice loud and rich until, sweating, tired and somewhat amazed at herself she came to rest with the words: 'I can't believe that was me'.

When I asked her what she had been imagining during the journey involving the cave, she said that she was protecting her young 'monster cubs' from being taken from her. As she said this she burst into tears, sobbing and crying on the words 'what happened to my children'.

The depth and severity of the pain which a woman such as Martha suffers is, for most of us, simply unimaginable. And, such pain can leave a person dumb, mute and exhausted. Yet, no matter how terrifying or overwhelming, this pain is better voiced. Nothing can enable Martha to mother her children, or walk, or drive a car or go rock-climbing again. But that does not mean that she needs to silence the magnitude of her feelings in response to what has befallen her.

As Martha cried, I returned to massaging and moving her torso, encouraging the voice tube to remain in Saxophone and helping her deepen the resonance of her sobs.

All the time I kept encouraging abdominal expansion, keeping her from leaning over and compressing the diaphragm.

Eventually she said: 'I don't think I have ever breathed so deeply or cried so loudly'. Then she let out a chuckle and said: 'What next?'.

Over the next period of our work together – about three months – we pursued a regular programme of work. First, we worked at keeping the sense of inner physical space expansive. Second, we encouraged the voice tube and upper respiratory tract to remain lengthened and dilated. Third, we explored Voice Movement Journeys which gave Martha an opportunity for authentic emotional release.

Through this work, we were able to reduce radically both the frequency and the severity of her asthma attacks as well as create the space for the artistic expression of psychological and physical pain through voice and movement.

Breathing the Cathartic Winds

Working with the breath tends to animate deep emotions and encourage what might be referred to as a cathartic release. There is something about drawing attention to the breath and amplifying the act of breathing that seems to disturb emotional stasis and activate affect with incredible immediacy and intensity. Add to this the dimension of voice, which also plays a releasing and expelling function, and you have a recipe for deep catharsis.

In some quarters during recent periods of western therapeutic history, catharsis through breathing and vocalising – particularly screaming – has been utilised within a paradigm which alleges that therapeutic benefit can be gained from the expression of extreme emotion through sound, accompanied by exaggerated breathing. In my opinion, such approaches only deal with part of the picture. For, though catharsis may be part of the journey towards recovery and self-knowledge, it is not enough on its own. In fact, on its own I think catharsis can actually be counter-productive. Because the issue of catharsis is always lurking close to vocal expression and breath work, I will in the next chapter investigate the bigger picture of therapeutic voicework generally and Voice Movement Therapy specifically, of which catharsis is a part.

CHAPTER 8

Voicing the Troubled Mind
Catharsis, Creativity and Recovery

Pain and Trauma

Many people seek therapeutic help of one kind or another because they reach a realisation that they can no longer carry the burden of intense psychological pain. This pain can take many forms: the pain of depression, the pain of sorrow, the pain of loneliness, the pain of panic, the pain of fear and the pain of anxiety. All these manifestations of pain take their toll on a person's psychological constitution and if they continue unabated they can create the sensation that the person lives in a traumatised state. Very often, psychological pain results in the first place from a specific trauma such as the trauma of bereavement, the trauma of sexual abuse or the trauma of a terrifying accident. In other circumstances, psychological pain may have accumulated in response to an ongoing traumatic situation, such as the trauma of an emotionally oppressive relationship.

Regardless of the particular manifestation of someone's hurt and whatever the particular causes of that hurt, therapeutically we are dealing with a person in pain and the role of the professional practitioner is to enable the person to experience relief from that pain and discover the healed Self.

The Sounds of Expressed Anguish

Each verbal and linguistic language has a different word for pain. Indeed, each language has a different word for sadness and happiness, for fear and panic, for love and hate, for joy and sorrow. Yet the vocal sounds which express such universal emotions are recognisable in every culture and in every society regardless of the language spoken.

When someone needs to express pain or anguish with authenticity and intensity, verbal language is of little use; for psychological pain emanates from a level of the psyche which is preverbal, transverbal and archetypal. An authentic expression of trauma necessitates vocal but non-verbal expression which means a return to an infantile mode of expression.

For the newly born infant, life after the 'birth trauma' is a series of 'little traumas': the trauma of sudden changes of temperature; the trauma of hunger; the trauma of abandonment when the mother leaves the room; the trauma of radical changes in acoustic environment as the ear adjusts to the impedance of air. And the psychological anguish which these traumas cause is expressed directly through vocal cries, wails and screams.

The preverbal infant does not translate or de-scribe his experience into a verbal culturally conditioned code; he gives direct expression to it through sound. However, once the child learns to speak, from that point on even the most intense emotional experiences will have to be named, worded and articulated in order to be communicated and accepted.

Yet for many people, the contents of the heart are simply beyond, beneath or above words. In addition to the burden of living with the trauma of unhealed pain, many people therefore face the further torment that their pain remains invisible because it cannot be spoken. For such people, providing an opportunity for vocal expression through sound offers an effective vehicle for healing.

Catharsis and Recovery

One of the oldest and most well-established models of mind–body functioning is the cathartic paradigm. According to a cathartic view, the human organism is a hydraulic system capable of receiving and dispensing energy. Energy enters and leaves the psychic and somatic system in a variety of ways. Energy can enter the body through the ears, so that when someone shouts at us, verbally abuses us or whispers sweet words of love to us, the energy in our system is increased. The same amount of energy may then be dispensed from our system if we verbally retaliate, punch our verbal aggressor or return the loving compliment with a kiss. Energy can also enter the system through the eyes. If we are exposed to a terrifying sight or if we set our eyes upon something of incredible beauty, then our psychic energy is increased. And this energy can be released through our behavioural reactions, such as running away screaming or singing the praises of the beauty which we behold.

The cathartic model proposes that to maintain health, the system must be kept in a state of energetic balance. Moreover, to keep the system in a state of balance, the same amount of energy which enters the system must in turn be released. However, there are many factors which prevent this from occurring: fear, intimidation, shock and a host of social prohibitions often prevent people from responding equally to the energetic events which influence them. As a result, a build-up of psychic energy occurs, causing an increase in pressure within the system.

Many people experience psychological pain because they have been traumatised either by a single event or by an ongoing situation; and the consequent pain is often the result of an accumulation of emotional energy which has not been discharged. A cathartic therapy is one which provides someone with an opportunity to discharge this accumulated energy in a safe place, as though reliving the original trauma but where the person is enabled to react to it and to retaliate.

When someone is offered an opportunity for catharsis, it is as though the emotional floodgates come bursting open and a historic backlog of unexpressed pain comes flowing out, leaving the person with a sense of having been relieved, perhaps even purged.

Voice and Catharsis

In order for a genuine catharsis to be facilitated, there has to be an open channel through which psychic energy can be released – and the voice provides such a channel.

The human voice is basically one long continuous tube which begins at the lips, becomes the mouth, curls down to become the throat, continues downwards into the neck becoming the larynx and travels on down into the chest where it splits into two tubes, one passing into each lung. There is then the sense that the voice is capable of bringing things up from deep inside the body.

Vocal catharsis involves allowing a person to vocalise a gamut of sounds which are emotionally charged and which depressurise the energetic system by discharging emotions which have hitherto remained contained. Such a process may be referred to as 'anti-singing'; that is to say that the person is taught to vocalise in such a way as to produce not the voice of beauty appropriate to the aesthetics of the concert hall but a voice which gives authentic acoustic form to pain through the non-beautiful voice. During a vocal cathartic process within Voice Movement Therapy the client may sob, wail, scream, bemoan, holler and screech as previously unexpressed trauma is given shape through sound. This means that the practitioner plays the role of a singing teacher, facilitating the client in acquiring a palette of sounds from which to draw when vocalising extreme emotional material.

Body Memory

One of the precepts of a cathartic model of therapy is that an excess of psychic energy which builds up in the system will eventually become localised in a particular part of the body where it is likely to manifest as a somatic illness, dysfunction or impedance. Intermittent headaches, skin rashes, disturbances of sight and hearing, stomach ulcers, digestive problems, frequent diarrhoea, aches in the skeletal muscles and major dysfunctions of the primary organs such as liver and kidneys have all been related to a psychogenic origin. This means that although the practitioner may be facilitating a cathartic discharge through vocal sound, the therapeutic process may also require that the practitioner work directly on the body with particular focus on an area around which the emotional energy associated with the accumulated trauma has constellated.

In cases where a part of the body somatises psychic pain, it is as though the body acts as a physical memory of a psychological trauma – what we may call a 'body memory'. Furthermore, the body is capable of remembering psychological trauma in the form of somatic pain, discomfort, disease or dysfunction even when the conscious mental memory appears to have forgotten the event or events which caused the trauma.

The word 'member' literally refers to a part of the body and to 're-member' means to put the body parts together in a particular way. When the body stores trauma, body parts are 're-membered' in a way that causes dysfunction and rectifying this requires that the therapist 'dis-members' the traumatised body. That is to say that the therapeutic process of 'dis-memberment' involves a loosening and a shaking free of the body's parts so that they can reconstellate or be 're-membered' afresh. Therefore, combined with the role of singing teacher, the Voice Movement Therapy practitioner also plays the role of masseur and physical therapist, manipulating the client's body to serve both the release of somatised emotion and the liberation of the body from constriction and pain.

For the client, this often involves the process of reliving the trauma physically, reinventing the postures and movements which would have accompanied the original event or events in order to follow them through to a positive conclusion. Indeed, Freud proposed that a cathartic therapy should give the client a second chance to react to the trauma in a way that was made impossible at the time (Freud 1953–74, Vol.3).

From Hurt to Healing

To be effective, a therapeutic process cannot end in a catharsis; and a process which uses voice as a primary channel of expression cannot end in the silence which follows the echo of vocalised pain. As the client discharges emotion through sound and movement it is paramount that the practitioner can seize the moment when sounds of anguish can become sounds of triumph, when sounds of intimidation can become sounds of victory, when sounds of horror can become sounds of joy and when sounds of grief can become sounds of hope.

One of the problems with a cathartic therapy is that the relief experienced can turn out to be short-lived and the psychic and somatic manifestation of trauma can quickly reconstellate as vigorously as before. This can lead to a cyclical dependency on some kind of cathartic release where the client is never really free from a repetitious return to an original hurt.

In my experience, in order for the cathartic relief to be long-lasting, the client must be enabled to take hold of the discharged emotion, transform it and, most important, make conscious expressive use of it. In this way, a certain artistic distance is created between the client as generator of emotional content and the client as a conscious sculptor of emotional form.

Artistic Distance

To understand the concept of 'artistic distance' and its therapeutic value it is useful to consider the art of the singer. In the course of an evening concert, a singer may sing a variety of emotionally charged songs from up-tempo light-hearted love songs to sorrowful ballads of desperation. In one song the singer may be beaming with a smile and genuinely feel full of glee as she sings; in the very next song the singer may weep and be genuinely full of sadness. Yet there is distance between the experience of emotion and the sculpturing of that emotion to form a song. Indeed, the song itself acts as a formed container for emotion which, otherwise, may pour endlessly from the voice without end.

If the singer is also the writer of her own songs, there may be a time, during the original writing of the song, when the singer is overwhelmed with emotion, particularly if she is drawing the song from her own traumatic experience. In many ways, the writing of the song may provide for a certain catharsis. But the art of the singer does not stop at this catharsis. The healing occurs in the next phase where the song can be sung with enough recollected authenticity of the original trauma to ensure an emotive realism but with enough distance to ensure that the rendition of the song is artful. This is what I have called 'artistic distance'.

One of the most important things which this artistic distance provides is the ability to reap pleasure from pain. For, the singer will experience the act of singing as highly pleasurable whilst at the same time experiencing something of the pain which the song may describe. Indeed, many singers will testify that the more painful the subject of the song the more pleasure is reaped from singing it. It is as though singing enables us to link arms with pain and remember its inevitable place in our life without finding our self immovably clasped by its grip.

Technique and Creativity

The client of a therapeutic process which uses voice as a primary medium, such as Voice Movement Therapy, may be compared to the singer. At first, a flood of sound is poured out, giving acoustic shape to deep emotion, very often of an extremely painful kind. But in time, this outpouring is familiar enough to be heard as the rudiments of a song and can be formed. It can be given melodic structure, rhythm and words. Meanwhile, the physical movements of the body which may be quite extreme and severe as they relive and recapitulate traumatic experiences can also be choreographed, until they take on the form of a dance.

At this point, the client is not only freed from a cycle of cathartic discharge but he is also, to a large extent, free of the interventions of the practitioner. The client can now move the body through space and guide the voice through the contours of the acoustic palette, creating an authentic song and dance from the fresh vitality which is uncovered by the release of pain – and the practitioner at this point is primarily a witness.

But it is this transition from the release of pain to the discovery of pleasure that presents the practitioner with the most difficult and sensitive task. In fact, in my opinion, facilitating the vocalisation of pain is a relatively straightforward procedure. But enabling that pain to be relinquished and reinvented in the form of a genuine healed Self requires great diligence, patience and sensitivity. For, if one attempts to heal pain too early, too quickly or too superficially, then the hurt Self feels patronised, belittled and poorly nursed and will, in an attempt to survive, persist all the more adamantly. On the other hand, if the hurt Self is encouraged to discharge itself continually without progression to an artistic mode of expression, the process of catharsis will serve only to feed the very pain that it seeks to heal.

In dealing with clients whose primary need is the expression and transformation of psychological pain, the Voice Movement Therapy practitioner is therefore in the combined role of psychotherapist, singing teacher and physical therapist. This means that the practitioner focuses simultaneously on a number of tasks. First, she must be able to offer a compassionate understanding of the client's expressions; second, she must be able to teach the client to release emotion through sound which balances authenticity of emotion with healthy use of the vocal instrument; third, she needs to be able to manipulate the client's body assisting the surmounting of somatised trauma; and fourth, she must be able to lead the client to a place of artistic distance from which the healed Self may experience a pleasure greater than the pain of the hurt Self. If the practitioner can combine these tasks, then a client suffering from the consequences of psychological pain can be offered a therapeutic process with genuine healing potential.

Let us return to Janice.

Case Study: Janice

Rape and Silence

Janice, whom I introduced earlier, was a professional musician. Her primary instrument is the French horn.

At the height of her career when she was enjoying success as a much sought-after player, Janice was consecutively raped by three men one night on her way home after a concert. Two of the three men took turns to hold her to the ground whilst the other raped her.

Despite the severe physical pain and the extreme emotional shock, Janice could barely make a sound throughout her ordeal. She tried to scream but could only produce a muffled shout. Whenever her voice did get anywhere near being loud enough to be heard, her oppressors covered her mouth with their hands.

As a result of her ordeal, Janice was unable to play with the orchestra for ten months, during which time she received counselling twice a week.

Since the ordeal she had suffered three main physical symptoms: a feeling that she had an iron bar running vertically down the centre of her torso, a feeling of constriction around the throat and constant breathlessness. In addition, her voice felt paralysed.

She came into therapy to try and regain some vocal strength and overcome the breathlessness but she also hoped for some further emotional healing in relation to the consequence of her having been raped.

When Janice vocalised it was in Flute with a great deal of free air. The sound also had a gentle vibrato which created the quality associated with someone who is nervous, perhaps even afraid. Janice said that when she vocalised, especially on a long continuous note, she felt the 'iron bar' tingling all the way down her chest.

As Janice vocalised over a period of about 15 minutes, I massaged the area vertically descending from the base of her neck to the pit of her stomach as well as the musculature each side of her spine. As I massaged and Janice vocalised, we both moved through Spherical Space in a dance which took its impulses from Janice's emotional journey.

Through this Voice Movement Massage, Janice went from fear, to rage, to triumph. At times she sobbed and shook, at times she yelled in despair and at other times she called out: 'Get away, get away'. As she called out these words: 'Get away', she held on to my arm with a vice-like grip, pulling me towards her.

When working with someone who has suffered the kind of trauma which Janice went through, the practitioner plays two roles in the fantasy of the client. First, in the case of Janice, being a man, I was in many ways representative of her assailants and during the session, Janice needed to identify me as the enemy in order to express her rage and anger vocally in a fashion that felt real. At the same time, I also represented the helper, the man that would save her from her assailants; she therefore needed to know that I would be there for her as she went through her intense experience.

As Janice called out: 'Get away, get away' and held on to my arm, I whispered to her: 'It's all right, I am right here'. At this point, she put her other hand on her chest and said that it was all tingling and going soft.

I asked her to lean over from the waist and imagine that the voice was pouring out of her like a liquid and she began vocalising in a series of long sounds like the siren on a ship. I asked her to imagine that she was singing down into a well and that her voice echoed in the open abyss. As she did this, I massaged her abdomen and in time, her voice opened into Saxophone. She was very hot and clammy and her breathing rate was very quick with the primary area of visible motility in the upper chest. I continued to massage her abdomen and encouraged her to breathe with abdominal expansion. This slowed down the breathing rate and increased the amount of inspired air.

Janice now came up to standing. Her face was red, her pupils were dilated and her hands and arms started thrashing about. As her arms gyrated, her voice whizzed round and round in siren-like sweeps. I placed my arms under hers and followed them about and it turned into a kind of martial arts dance. Janice began to make 'karate-like' movements with her arms and her voice took on an aggressive quality, punctuated with rhythmic bursts.

I now stood back and moved to her front where we could make eye contact. She said: 'I want to go up – can I?' I said: 'Of course' and she started ascending the pitch range in Saxophone going all the way up to a piercing whistle which she sustained for about a minute before breathing and repeating it again. The piercing whistle-like scream went on and on as though it would never stop.

As she vocalised, I asked her to imagine that she was a great white bird, flying above the cool pacific sea, swooping and gliding, like a mythical creature from Wagner, and asked her to improvise a melody in this ultra-high range. She began to sing in a voice so clear and so high it would have made the audience at Covent Garden fall from their seats.

Her arm movements became wing movements and her voice whistled on.

Then I asked her to continue singing imagining that she was a bird of prey, swooping in her search for food. I wanted her to stop and settle on the ground, but she would not.

Eventually, Janice came to stillness and I asked her to continue vocalising and go down through Primate, into Feline-canine, over onto her side and then onto her back.

She later told me that she was terrified that if she got onto her back on the floor her voice would go again and she would not be able to move. She was afraid of finding herself back in the paralysed silence of the rape again.

Janice vocalised and went down through the cycle. As she rolled over onto her back, her legs went up in the air, her arms gyrated and tore the air to shreds and her voice reached its crescendo. Then she leapt up onto her feet, sang out and fell back down to the floor again, rolling over onto her back. She went round and round this cycle, proving to herself that she could vocalise fully and move freely from the position she had been raped in to a triumphant standing position.

When she stopped, I asked Janice to take some time to sit and write a stream of words which expressed her experience and told her that we would use the words as the lyrics to a song.

She returned with:

> The iron in my chest
> The rage in my heart
> The blood in my cunt
> The poison in their eyes
> The sorrow in my soul
> The danger in my trust
> The ending of this tale
> Has now become a must
> Listen to my voice
> And let me live again

We now returned to vocalising in the high whistle in Saxophone which she had discovered, but this time she sang the words – like a diva.

This was the beginning of a series of songs which Janice wrote during her Voice Movement Therapy sessions, and the songs became a map by which she plotted her journey to recovery.

Using Voice and Song in Therapy

The case of Janice exemplifies the way that the methodology of Voice Movement Therapy develops from elementary physical and respiratory work into creative writing and the use of song. Of course, in a therapeutic relationship with a client, the practitioner may move back and forth between creative work through writing and singing and physical work through movement and massage. For the purpose of convenience, however, I have concentrated primarily on the physical aspects of Voice Movement Therapy in this book. But the part of Voice Movement Therapy which uses creative song-writing and singing as a therapy is the subject of the next volume in this series, *Using Voice and Singing in Therapy: The Practical Application of Voice Movement Therapy*; and in that book I shall return to the story of Janice as an example of how singing and song-making has the power to yield psychological growth.

The Voice Movement Therapy System of Vocal Analysis

The Vocal Analysis System

Component One: Pitch

> Each vocal sound is perceived to have a certain pitch, note or fundamental tone, determined by the frequency of vocal cord vibration. This is perceived within the metaphor of high to low, though in fact does not relate to spatial dimensions but to speed of vibration in time.

The initial sound which is shaped and coloured to produce a unique human voice is made by the vibration of the vocal cords. These two folds of tissue, also known as the vocal folds, lie stretched out in the larynx. At the front they are attached to the Adam's apple or thyroid cartilage and at the back they are connected to two movable cartilages called the arytenoids.

These two pieces of tissue are further attached to the trachea and the surrounding inner walls of the larynx by a complex set of muscles known collectively as the intrinsic laryngeal musculature. During normal breathing the vocal folds lie at rest, one each side of the larynx, like an open pair of curtains allowing air to pass freely through a window. The hole between the vocal folds through which air passes is called the glottis. However, adjustments in the distribution of tension in the laryngeal musculature can cause the vocal folds to close, preventing air from entering or leaving the trachea, like a thick pair of curtains drawn tightly shut across a window.

The sound of the human voice is generated by the rapid and successive opening and closure of the vocal cords many times per second and it is to this process that people refer when they speak of the vibration of the vocal cords. This rapid vibration of the vocal cords causes the expelled air from the lungs to be released through the glottis in a series of infinitesimal puffs which create a sound wave.

The faster the vocal cords vibrate, the higher the pitch. The slower they vibrate, the lower the pitch. As a useful point of reference, to sing middle C, the vocal cords must vibrate about 256 times per second. To sing the A above middle C they must vibrate at around 440 times per second.

Because the vocal folds are attached front and back to the thyroid and arytenoid cartilages, which are in turn connected to muscle tissue, they can be stretched out by tensile adjustment in the laryngeal musculature making them longer, thinner and more tense. When this happens, like all elastic objects which are tightened, they vibrate at a higher frequency which produces a higher sound or pitch. Conversely, an alternative adjustment of the laryngeal musculature causes the vocal folds to slacken, so that they become shorter, thicker and more lax. When this happens, like all elastic objects which are relaxed, they vibrate at a lower frequency and the consequent sound of the voice deepens in pitch.

In establishing a component system of intuitive vocal analysis, the first physiologically generated component of perceivable acoustic sound which we can identify as being present in a person's voice is therefore the pitch, also referred to as the note or the tone.

Component Two: Pitch Fluctuation

The pitch of the voice sustains more or less constancy or fluctuation in a given time. This is determined by the shifting frequencies of vocal cord vibration.

During vibration, the vocal cords may not remain absolutely constant in their speed of vibration over a given time and consequently they may produce a pitch fluctuation.

There are two components to this pitch fluctuation: interval distance and time. Interval distance is the magnitude of the pitch fluctuation. For example, a voice which fluctuates from a vibrational frequency of 440 to 450 times per second makes a pitch fluctuation across a tiny interval from the A above middle C on a piano to a sound not even high enough to sound the A-sharp above it. A voice meanwhile which fluctuates from 440 to 493 times per second makes a pitch fluctuation across a large interval equivalent to going from the A above middle C on the piano to the B above it. The term 'interval' thereby denotes the magnitude of the frequency jump between two specific notes or pitches.

The next factor, time, is the speed with which the fluctuations are made. A very slow alternation between 440 times per second, which is the A above middle C on the piano and 450 times per second, which does not have a note on the piano, may well sound 'out of tune' to a listener. But if the same inconsistency is quickened it may sound like a very professional singing voice. Indeed, very fast fluctuations in vocal cord vibration over a very small pitch interval constitute what is known as vibrato, that deliberate flutter which is heard in the classical European voice. If a singer produces such pitch fluctuations too slowly, or takes them across too great a pitch interval, the skill of the vibrato turns into what we hear as untuneful singing.

The second vocal component parameter which we can identify within the human voice then is pitch fluctuation which under certain conditions would be referred to as vibrato and under others may be called inconsistency or untunefulness. However, what is heard as pleasant and unpleasant, as an acceptable interval, and an unacceptable interval is culturally determined.

Component Three: Loudness

> The human voice is perceived on a spectrum of loudness from quiet through moderate to loud. Loudness is determined by how hard the two vocal cords contact each other during vibration which is in turn primarily determined by the pressure of breath released from the lungs.

Increased pressure of breath expelled from the lungs draws the vocal folds together with a greater force causing them to hit each other with higher impact. Decreased air pressure, meanwhile, draws the folds together with less force, causing them to hit each other with low impact. We witness this concept when watching or listening to a pair of drawn curtains flap together during a high wind. As the pressure of the wind against the curtains increases so they flap together with greater impact, giving off a louder sound. Conversely, as the wind dies down, the curtains hit one another more gently, making the sound softer.

To increase the air pressure and therefore the loudness, we increase the contractile power of the muscles around the torso. To decrease pressure and loudness we ease off the muscular contraction.

The third vocal component which we can identify in a human voice then is loudness which results from increased air pressure.

Component Four: Glottal Attack

> The voice is perceived as having greater or lesser attack, determined by the impact under which the vocal folds come together during phonation.

Unlike curtains, the vocal cords are not only reliant upon the wind from the lungs for their movement as they are connected to muscles which are fed by nerves. It is therefore possible to vary the impact of vocal cord contact without major changes in air pressure, increasing and decreasing vocal cord impact, creating sounds with varying degrees of glottal attack whilst maintaining a constant loudness.

The fourth component parameter of vocal sound which we can identify is therefore glottal attack, determined by the impact of vocal fold contact.

Component Five: Free Air

> The quality of the voice is perceived as being more or less breathy or airy, perceived on a spectrum from none through moderate to high and determined by the volume or quantity of air flowing through the glottis.

Although the vocal cords are opening and closing very quickly, they may not push tightly together when they close. If the vocal cords are closed, but are not kept pushed together tightly, then even during their closed phase, air can pass through the folds in the form of a trickle or a seepage. When this happens the voice has a certain breathiness which is described as a voice rich in free air. A voice may also be rich in free air if the glottis is enlarged during vocal cord vibration.

The fifth component of the voice is therefore free air which is perceived on a spectrum from little through moderate to high.

Component Six: Disruption

> The human voice may or may not be to some degree disrupted, that is broken or sporadically interrupted in a way which appears to interfere with the continuity of the tone. This can be caused by friction or uneven contact between the vocal folds, by other tissue structures coming into contact with the vocal cords during vibration or by intermittent silence breaking up the tone.

We have so far assumed that during vocalisation the vocal folds are drawn together so as to meet flush and smooth along their vibrating edge, preventing air to escape other than during their rhythmic opening and thereby producing a clear tone. However, under certain circumstances, not only may the vocal folds not meet under enough pressure to prevent air escaping, but also the vocal folds may crash together unevenly, their edges being corrugated and uneven, rubbing against each other and producing a sound which sounds broken, frictional, rough and discontinuous. These broken sounds are referred to as disrupted.

At other times, such as during laryngitis or influenza or when the vocal cords are damaged, the vocal tone may be intermittently broken with silences. In addition, other tissue structures in the larynx may come into contact with the vocal cords during vocalisation, interrupting the tone.

The sixth vocal component parameter which we can identify within the human voice is therefore disruption.

Component Seven: Register

> The voice is produced with what is perceived as a certain register, either modal, falsetto, whistle or vocal fry. The voice can also be perceived as being composed of a blended combination of modal and falsetto.

If a person begins to sing the lowest note possible and rises one note at a time up to the highest he or she can sing, it will be possible to discern alterations in the timbre at certain points, as though the person has 'changed voices'. Among the changes which a listener would observe would be a shift of 'register'.

Most voices have two main registers in singing, known as modal and falsetto. The most familiar and easily recognisable change between the modal and falsetto registers occurs when a man or a woman ascends upwards from a deep pitch towards higher ones during which at a certain point a 'register break' occurs where the voice 'breaks' out of modal and into falsetto. It is this register break which is exaggerated and musicalised in the yodelling style of singing originating in Switzerland. In classical European singing, singers learn to blend the two registers together so that the break is not heard.

Scientific instrumentational investigation has not yet been able to explain exactly what does cause the audible shifts in timbre which give rise to particular registers. We do know, however, that the alterations in the size of the glottis are instrumental in effecting change in what is known as voice register.

Both modal and falsetto register can be produced on low and high pitches, though the higher the voice in pitch the more natural and easier it is to produce falsetto and the lower the pitch of the voice the more natural and easier it is to produce modal. In addition, through precise control of the laryngeal musculature, a vocal sound can be produced which blends together the two registers into a single quality.

If the vocal folds remain closed along the majority of their length so that only a minimal portion is vibrating, making a tiny glottis, the voice quality produced is like a piercing scream and is known as the whistle register. Because this requires extreme tension in the vocal folds, the pitch of the whistle register is always very high. If, in contradistinction, the vocal folds are very lax and their entire length is vibrating then the quality of voice often produced is like a low, airy grumble known as the vocal fry register which, due to the lack of tension in the folds, is always produced on low notes.

The seventh component to vocal sound which we can therefore identify is vocal register, of which the two main ones are modal and falsetto with two less frequently heard registers named whistle and vocal fry.

Component Eight: Violin

The human voice may be heard as possessing a spectral degree of nasal resonance from none through moderate to high. When nasal resonance is severely inhibited or blocked, the sound may metaphorically be described as lacking in violin; when nasal resonance is full, the voice may be described as possessing a high degree of violin.

Some of the sound wave created by the vibrating vocal cords may pass through the nasal passage which runs from the oro-pharynx up above the roof of the mouth and out through the nose and the amount of air which passes through this tract influences the vocal quality. The passage of air through the nasal tube can be controlled by the raising and lowering of the soft palate, which closes and opens the port of entry to the nasal tract. At one extreme, the movement of air through this passage can be completely prevented and at the other, the maximum amount of air capable of passing through this port can travel through the nasal passages and out of the nose. Between these two extremes, an entire spectrum of nasal air flow is possible.

When the soft palate is lowered allowing maximum nasal resonance, the voice is described as possessing a lot of violin. When the soft palate is closed so that nasal resonance is inhibited, the voice is described as lacking in violin.

The eighth vocal component of the human voice which we can identify is therefore the degree of nasal resonance which is given the instrumental and metaphorical name of 'violin' and perceived on a spectrum from none through moderate to high.

Component Nine: Harmonic Resonance – Flute, Clarinet, Saxophone

> Harmonic timbre is the particular quality of the voice determined by the shape and dimensions of the vocal tract or voice tube. Harmonic timbre may be arbitrarily divided into three qualities arising from a short narrow tract, a medium length and diameter tract and a fully lengthened and dilated tract. These are given the names 'Flute', 'Clarinet' and 'Saxophone' respectively.

The vocal tract which runs upwards from the larynx, becomes the pharynx, turns into the oro-pharynx and curls round to become the mouth is capable of altering its size and shape. And, it is the shape and movement of this tube which governs so much of the specific quality of a voice which we hear, regardless of the degree and combination of the eight component parameters hitherto identified.

To understand how the movement and configuration of this tube affects vocal quality it will be useful to imagine three crude tubes, closed at the bottom but open at the top, all made of exactly the same substance but constructed to different diameters and different lengths. The first is short and narrow; the second is relatively longer and wider; and the third is much longer and more dilated again. Imagine that we hold a tuning fork which produces middle C over the top of each tube in turn and listen to the sound of the note echoing or resonating inside the tubes. In moving from listening to the sound inside the first tube to the same note echoing or resonating in the second and then the third, the listener would hear a change of timbre. Probably, the first tube would sound more comparable to a flute, the second tube would sound more comparable to the clarinet, whilst the sound produced by the third tube would sound more akin to the saxophone; they would all however sound the note C.

With regard to voice production, both the length and the diameter of the voice tube or vocal tract can alter, producing a variety of timbres, yet the pitch can be held constant by an unchanging frequency of vocal cord vibration. So, imagine that instead of a tuning fork at the top of three crude tubes, you have vibrating vocal cords at the bottom of one tube which can change its length and diameter to assume the relative dimensions of all three tubes. This gives some idea of how different timbres are created by the vocal instrument.

The vocal tract which runs downwards from the lips to the larynx is an elastic tube which can assume various lengths and diameters.

In place of the three crude tubes, we can now therefore pinpoint three arbitrary degrees of dilation and lengthening along the path of the vocal tract. The first compares to a flute-like tube, whereby the larynx is high in the neck and the tract is quite constricted creating a short, narrow tube, such as when we blow a kiss or whistle. The second configuration, which compares to the clarinet-like tube, is characterised by a lower position of the larynx in the neck creating a longer tube which is more dilated, such as when we steam up a pair of glasses. The third configuration, which compares to the saxophone-like tube, is characterised by a complete descent of the larynx in the neck, creating a long tube with maximum dilation, such as when we yawn.

If the vibratory frequency of the vocal cords is maintained at a constant, say at 256 times per second, producing middle C, whilst the vocal tract moves from Flute Configuration through Clarinet Configuration to Saxophone Configuration, the effect will be to sing the same note with three very distinct timbres, comparable to that achieved when playing the note C on a tuning fork held above the three separate crude tubes imagined earlier.

In Voice Movement Therapy, we give the vocal timbre produced by a short narrow voice tube the instrumental name Flute Timbre; we name the vocal timbre produced by a medium length and diameter tube Clarinet Timbre; and we call the vocal timbre produced by a fully lengthened and dilated voice tube Saxophone Timbre.

Component Ten: Articulation

The human voice may be perceived as producing sounds which are usable within the spoken language of a particular culture and which are produced by the shapes of the vocal tract in combination with the movements of tongue and lips.

It is the harmonic embellishment of a pitch caused by changing dimensions of the vocal tract which gives rise to specific timbres which we call vowels and which are born from very specific shapes of the vocal tract.

In addition, the air flow from the larynx may be momentarily stopped. Sometimes the air is stopped at the back of the mouth, such as 'k'. Other consonants are produced by interrupting the air flow at the lips, such as 'p' or 'b'. Some articulate sounds are used in one language but not in another. For example, 'ach' is used in German and Arabic but not in English.

The tenth and last vocal component or parameter is therefore articulation, composed of vowels and consonants.

The Ten Vocal Components

From a simple understanding of vocal physiology it is therefore possible to deduce ten elements which combine to form the sound of the human voice. When listening to a person vocalising, whether in song, or in speech, whether in a therapeutic or a creative context, a practitioner can be trained to listen to the voice in terms of these components which provide the basis for interpretation, analysis and training. These components of vocal expression form the core of a system of Voicework which is both an analytic profile for interpreting voices, a psychotherapeutic means by which to investigate the way psychological material is communicated through specific vocal qualities, a training system for developing the expressiveness of voices and a physiotherapeutic means by which to release the voice from functional misuse.

I have presented extensive recordings of the ten vocal components with a detailed explanation of the Voice Movement Therapy System of Vocal Analysis on a set of audio tapes, *The Singing Cure: Liberating Self Expression Through Voice Movement Therapy* (Newham 1998).

To recap, here are the ten components:

Component One: Pitch

Each vocal sound is perceived to have a certain pitch, note or fundamental tone, determined by the frequency of vocal cord vibration. This is perceived within the metaphor of high to low, though in fact does not relate to spatial dimensions but to speed of vibration in time.

Component Two: Pitch Fluctuation

The pitch of the voice sustains more or less constancy or fluctuation in a given time. This is determined by the shifting frequencies of vocal cord vibration.

Component Three: Loudness

The human voice is perceived on a spectrum of loudness from quiet through moderate to loud. Loudness is determined by how hard the two vocal cords contact each other during vibration which is in turn primarily determined by the pressure of breath released from the lungs.

Component Four: Glottal Attack

The voice is perceived as having greater or lesser attack, determined by the impact under which the vocal folds come together during phonation.

Component Five: Free Air

The quality of the voice is perceived as being more or less breathy or airy, perceived on a spectrum from none through moderate to high and determined by the volume or quantity of air flowing through the glottis.

Component Six: Disruption

The human voice may or may not be to some degree disrupted, that is broken or sporadically interrupted in a way which appears to interfere with the continuity of the tone. This can be caused by friction or uneven contact between the vocal folds, by other tissue structures coming into contact with the vocal cords during vibration or by intermittent silence breaking up the tone.

Component Seven: Register

The voice is produced with what is perceived as a certain register, either modal, falsetto, whistle or vocal fry. The voice can also be perceived as being composed of a blended combination of modal and falsetto.

Component Eight: Violin

The human voice may be heard as possessing a spectral degree of nasal resonance from none through moderate to high. When nasal resonance is severely inhibited or blocked, the sound may metaphorically be described as lacking in violin; when nasal resonance is full, the voice may be described as possessing a high degree of violin.

Component Nine: Harmonic Resonance – Flute, Clarinet, Saxophone

Harmonic timbre is the particular quality of the voice determined by the shape and dimensions of the vocal tract or voice tube. Harmonic timbre may be arbitrarily divided into three qualities arising from a short narrow tract, a medium length and diameter tract and a fully lengthened and dilated tract. These are given the names 'Flute', 'Clarinet' and 'Saxophone' respectively.

Component Ten: Articulation

The human voice may be perceived as producing sounds which appear close to a sound usable within the spoken language of a particular culture and which are produced by the shapes of the vocal tract in combination with the movements of tongue and lips.

Further Information

For further information including a list of qualified Voice Movement Therapy practitioners, a full prospectus of trainings and courses and a complete list of currently available resources including the accompanying video and set of audio tapes, please contact:

The Administrator
Voice Movement Therapy
PO Box 4218
London
SE22 0JE
Tel: +44 (0) 181 693 9502
Fax: +44 (0) 181 299 6127
Email: info@voicework.com

Information can also be accessed on the Voice Movement Therapy web site: www.voicework.com

References

Benjamin, A. (1993) 'In search of integrity.' *Dance Theatre Journal 10*, 4, 42–46.

Benjamin, A. (1995) 'Unfound movement.' *Dance Theatre Journal 12*, 1, 44–47.

Farmer, P. (1972) *Tarzan Alive: A Definitive Biography of Lord Greystoke.* New York: Doubleday.

Fossey, D. (1983) *Gorillas in the Mist.* Boston: Houghton Mifflin.

Freud, S. (1953–74) *Standard Edition of the Complete Psychological Works of Sigmund Freud.* Ed. James Strachey. London: Hogarth Press.

Jung, C.G. (1953) *Collected Works of C. G. Jung.* (Bollingen Series XX.) H. Read, M. Fordham, G. Adler and W. McGuire (eds). Princeton University Press and London: Routledge and Kegan Paul.

Kessler, I. (1997) 'Sounding Our Way to Wholeness: Linking the Metaphorical and Physical Voice in a Pilot Study with Women Using Breath, Voice and Movement.' Unpublished doctoral thesis, Union Institute College of Graduate Studies.

Newham, P. (1997a) *Shouting for Jericho: The Work of Paul Newham on the Human Voice.* Video. London: Tigers Eye/Class Productions.

Lofting, H. (1950) *The Voyages of Dr. Doolittle.* Philadelphia: Lippincott.

Newham, P. (1997a) *Shouting for Jericho: The Work of Paul Newham on the Human Voice.* London: Tiger's Eye/Class Productions.

Newham, P. (1997b) *Therapeutic Voicework: Principles and Practice for the Use of Singing as a Therapy.* London: Jessica Kingsley Publishers.

Newham. P. (1998) *The Singing Cure: Liberating Self Expression Through Voice Movement Therapy.* Audio cassettes. Boulder: Sounds True.

Index